IN PURPOSE, NOT ON PURPOSE

Mini Series
Three Stories in One

*La*Tasha *B*rooks

PAGE PUBLISHING, INC.
New York, NY

First originally published by Page Publishing, Inc. 2019

ISBN 978-1-64462-645-0 (Paperback)
ISBN 978-1-64462-646-7 (Digital)

Printed in the United States of America

Dedication

I would like to first and foremost give Glory to God.

Then, I have to give a shout out to my past, present and future, it is in His hands.

To all who have lost hope or their way at some point in their lives just know, that when you serve a sovereign God all things will work together for Great.

I love you Husband "Money", Renee, Gma Ann, Aunt Ingrid, Jeffrey Jr., Jekeyseon, Jelayza, T'oni, Bra'Zya, Brandon Jr., Ja'Niyah, Erica, Kim, Keisha, Felisha, Shequila, Mesha, Erica B.

R.I.P Grandma Wanda and My heart beat, Dad "Jason"

The Monster

Rat Race

My mom, my two little sisters, and I were sitting in the car. My mom was snapping her fingers to a song that was playing on the radio. My sisters and I were sitting in the back seat laughing at our mom. Our giggles and chuckles were interrupted when my mom bolted out the words "WHAT THE FUCK!" I looked up to see what she was reacting to. I saw a mob of men running from a mile away. They were headed in the direction of our car. The closer they got, I noticed that De'Lye was leading the pack. He ran faster than I ever saw him run. He had a look on his face that looked like he saw a ghost. He looked like he was in fear for his life. The mob of men was maybe two yards behind him. I could tell he got an early start, or he was just a super-fast runner. At first I thought they were with him, but the closer they got, I realized they were chasing him.

The Getaway

My mom quickly flung open the passenger door and jumped from the passenger side to the driver side of the car. She turned the keys that were already left in the ignition. My eyes stayed fixated on the mob of men. "Why were they chasing him?" I wondered. When De'Lye reached the car, he jumped in fast slamming and locking the door behind him. My mom put the car in drive, and we sped away like we were on a high-speed chase. I looked back in the back window at the mob of angry men. They were becoming more distant the further we drove. I noticed something, all of the guys that were chasing De'Lye had familiar faces. I recognized all of them. De'Lye turned around to the back seat and yelled, "THIS IS YOUR FAULT!" He raised his hand to strike me, but my mom grabbed his hand. She looked him in the eyes with a dead set stare and yelled, "DON'T!"

My Mom's Boyfriend

We stayed in the 12th Street projects. De'Lye came to visit my mom and us. De'Lye and my mom were in the early stages of dating. De'Lye lived in a little town outside of Austin, Texas, called Waco, Texas. He would come down to Austin to visit us every other weekend. My sisters and I were upstairs playing and coloring. My mom and De'Lye were downstairs watching television. There was a knock on the door that echoed through the entire house. The knock was louder than any other knock I'd heard before. I was always inquiring. My mom called it nosy. When I heard the knock, I ran down the stairs. I wanted to see who was knocking on the door. De'Lye was sitting on the couch.

A Knock at the Door

My mom was answering the front door. Before my mom could get the door open, some guy barged his way into the door. I didn't recognize him. He looked angry about something. When he barged in the door, his eyes scrolled the room. They stopped at De'Lye sitting on the couch. Then he looked back at my mom and yelled, "WHO THE FUCK IS THIS NIGGA?" Mom didn't say anything. She had a look of worry and confusion on her face. De'Lye looked more confused and worried than she did. Then he stood up to his feet and said, "Who are you, nigga? You don't know me?" The man walked to my mom's side. My mom was still standing by the front door. It looked as if she wanted to run out of the front door to get away from both of the guys. The man rushed back to my mom's side, put his right arm around her back to her right shoulder. Then he put his left arm around the front of her chest, reaching to her right shoulder from the front. He squeezed her in a hugging manner. He said, "This is my fucking woman. She is about to have my baby." My mouth dropped because I had never seen the man before.

The Trash Talker

The man continued saying things and talking trash to De'Lye. It was as if he was trying to provoke him to anger. The man began speaking on private encounters that he and my mom had. De'Lye stayed nonchalant. I could tell that he was soaking it all in. De'Lye appeared to be unbothered. However, his nose was flaring. He didn't say anything at all. The man babbled on so much. I don't think De'Lye could've gotten a word in if he tried to. Unexpectedly, my mom called out the man's name. She said, "Squeaky." I thought to myself, I heard her mention that name before. I was always eavesdropping in on her conversations. I remember her telling her sister that she liked Squeaky, but she liked De'Lye better. She said she had to end things with Squeaky. Well, I would assume ending things with Squeaky didn't go so well 'cause now here we were. Squeaky continued running his mouth on and on. I don't think he heard my mom call his name. My mom called his name for the second time, and he still did not hear. For the third time, with more aggression and frustration, my mom yelled. She said, "SQUEAKY! YOU NEED TO GET OUT OF MY HOUSE!"

His Surprise

Squeaky gave my mom a look of astonishment. He probed deeply into her eyes as if he was searching for something. My mom met gaze with him for a moment, and she turned away. Squeaky said, "But you are about to have my child." My mom said, "Not anymore." Squeaky said, "What does that mean?" My mom said, "Just go." Squeaky was not trying to go back out the door from which he came. De'Lye abruptly charged Squeaky. De'Lye grabbed Squeaky by the shirt. De'Lye began charging Squeaky out of the front door. I don't think Squeaky was prepared for that. It seemed as if he didn't resist when he was being thrown out of the front door. As De'Lye was charging him out of the front door, he was talking to him. He said, "Didn't she tell you to get out of her house? You a hardheaded ass nigga." My mom ran to the front door. I followed her. Then she stepped outside to stand on the porch. By this time De'Lye and Squeaky were on the sidewalk beneath where the last step to the porch ended. Squeaky's eyes wondered upward toward my mom, who was still standing on the porch. When he saw her standing on the porch, either his demeanor changed, or he got a surge of testosterone. Squeaky grabbed De'Lye hand and threw them off his shirt.

A Brawl

Then he punched De'Lye in the face. De'Lye's lip began to bleed. De'Lye balled his fist and extended his arm to punch Squeaky. Before De'Lye could extend his arm in full to connect a punch to Squeaky's face, my mom rushed off the porch and started throwing punches at Squeaky. She was screaming, "Leave him alone. Leave him alone!" They were like professional tag teamers. They rumbled and rolled three or four-yard sticks away from the front porch. They ended up in the grass against the back wall of one of our neighbor's apartment. I stayed on the porch watching from afar. Then something in me made me feel like there was something I needed to be doing to protect my mother. I ran upstairs to one of our other neighbor's house. I banged on the door until someone answered. A guy from our projects opened the door. His name was Bubba. I wasn't expecting him to answer. I was looking for the person that lived there. Her name was Mrs. JoJo. When Bubba answered the door, he said, "Hey, Ty." I said, "Hi. Where is Mrs. JoJo?" Bubba opened the door wider. I met eyes with a woman sitting on the couch. It was Mrs. JoJo. I rushed over to Mrs. JoJo. I asked, "Mrs. JoJo, will you please give me a knife?" She said, "Honey, you are six years old. What do you need a knife for?" I said, "Because my mom and De'Lye are outside fighting some man named Squeaky. I need to help my mom." Mrs. JoJo said, "Honey, you don't need a knife."

Break Up That Fight

Then she turned to Bubba and said, "Bubba, go out there and break up that fight." Bubba instantly went out the door to break up the fight. My mom, De'Lye, and Squeaky were nowhere to be found, but everyone in the projects was outside. They were drawn to drama and commotion. Everyone was following the fight. My mom, De'Lye, and Squeaky had made it all the way around to the park area. That was the length of another small complex building. I continued following Bubba until we saw my mom and De'Lye. The cops were there taking statements from all parties involved. When I saw my mom, she told me to go back around to the house. I went back to the house. I went inside the house where my sisters where. They were still upstairs playing with toys and coloring. I continued playing with dolls and coloring.

My Cousins

Shortly after, my mom and De'Lye made it back home. They talked more about the situation, but she made sure I stayed in the room with my sisters, and the doors remained shut. I don't know what they discussed, but from that day forward, I didn't hear the name Squeaky mentioned again. I never saw him again. De'Lye was at our apartment all the time. My sisters and I enjoyed De'Lye being there. He was nice to us. Two months passed from the time of the altercation, my mom's sister planned on going out of town for a week or so. My aunt asked my mom if she could take care of her children for two weeks. My mom agreed. I loved having my cousin there at the apartment with us. We all attended the same school. It was fun for them to have us all go to school together from the same house. Besides, my two little sisters were in daycare. They were not old enough to attend the school that my cousins and I were attending. They went to school with me from our apartment from Monday until Friday. When we went to school on Friday, we were excited about the next day which was the weekend. We wanted to go to the park to play. When the school bell rang, we all met up at the normal after school pick up spot. My mom, her sister, or my grandma would pick us up. On this day, De'Lye picked us all up from school.

The Walk Home

He wasn't in a car. He was on foot. De'Lye walked us all home. Our apartment was three or four blocks away from our school. We enjoyed walking and talking with De'Lye. I asked De'Lye where my mom was. He said, "She had some business to take care of. After she was done taking care of business, she would be home soon." The walk home took us approximately fifteen minutes. Once we made it to the front door of the apartment, De'Lye pulled my mom's necklace keychain off his neck. He fondled through a set of keys until he came to the gold house key. He opened the apartment door to let us all into the apartment. We were excited to go outside and play. I ran upstairs to put my backpack in my room. My cousins followed. When we came back down the stairs, I asked, "De'Lye, where were my little sisters?" He said, "They are with ya mama." I said, "Oh okay. Can we go to the park?" He said, "Yes, just come back in the house before the street lights come on." We all said, "OKAY!" My two cousins and I took off running out the door. De'Lye ran to the door to catch us before we got out of range. He yelled, "AND Y'ALL BETTER COME BACK TOGETHER." He sounded just like our mom and grandma. He had the routine down packed.

The Playground

We started our journey towards the park. We played and had fun with each other and all the other kids in the projects. The park was packed with kids. It was always packed on Friday after school until 6pm Sunday. We played until the street lights came on. When it was time to go, we could not find my cousin Elijah. Elijah was the oldest of all three of us. I was second and Kymara was third. Kymara and I went to the bathroom area, and we knocked on a few apartment doors to some of our friends, that lived closer to the park area. I remembered Elijah telling me she had to use the bathroom. I assumed she was going to use the park bathroom. I was having so much fun playing with so many kids that I did not realize if Elijah came back to the park. Kymara and I were afraid to go home because we all know we are supposed to stick together. That had always been implanted in us ever since we were babies. It was getting darker and darker. Kymara and I decided to go ahead and go home.

Elijah Went Missing

We just knew we were going to get in trouble for not having Elijah with us. When we made it to the front door of the house, I told Kymara to knock on the door of the apartment we stayed in. While she was knocking on our door, I was going to run up the stairs to Mrs. JoJo apartment to see if she'd seen Elijah. Kymara didn't knock. She turned the knob and walked into the apartment. The door was unlocked. Kymara was in the apartment for less than a minute before she ran back out. I was at the top of the stairs when I looked to my right to see Kymara ran back out. I saw the look on Kymara's face that was not normal. I ran back down the stairs. I said, "What? What happened? Did you find Elijah?" Kymara said, "Elijah pulled De'Lye's dick out his pants." I said, "What?" I was so shocked because none of us could say curse words.

Private Parts

We would always call private parts little pet names. We called the penis a ding dong and the vagina was a coochie or a tutu. The only thing I heard was DICK. Then I had to think about and put together what it was that she was telling me and then I visualized Elijah pulling De'Lye's penis out his pants. We were too young to know or even think in that manner. De'Lye was a stand-up guy. Maybe Kymara was confused, I thought. I just couldn't understand or make sense of what she was telling me. So, I asked her what did De'Lye do when she did that. Kymara said, "Nothing. He just let her." I was like, "Huh?" I walked into the house. Kymara followed. Elijah was sitting on De'Lye's lap, messing with the hair on his face. I didn't see her pull his dick out, but I believed Kymara. After that moment, we didn't talk about what had just occurred.

The Move

My mom arrived a couple of hours later with my two little sisters. After eating and bathing, we went to bed like it was a normal night. The next day, I woke to find that my cousins were gone. I asked my mom, "Where is Kymara and Elijah?" She said, "Their mama came to pick them up." I said, "Oh okay." I noticed that my mom and De'Lye were boxing up all our things. They emptied out the cabinet's drawers and put everything in boxes. I asked her what we were doing. She said, "We are moving." I said, "Where?" She said, "Out of town. To a bigger place." It took us all day to get the entire house packed up. De'Lye and my mom moved all the big items into a moving truck. All the items that did not fit into the truck, we packed up in the trunk of my mom's car. My mom, De'Lye, my sisters, and I loaded up in the car. We headed to De'Lye's hometown. We were driving for fifty-five minutes, and I fell asleep. My sisters were sleeping the first thirty minutes of driving.

Dottie's

I woke the next morning in a foreign place. The bed I was laying in was big and nice. My two little sisters were laying in the same bed with me. Before I could get a glimpse of the entire room, my sense of smell was intensified. Something smelled so good and familiar. What was that smell? It was so aromatic. Then I figured out the smell. It was the smell of bacon. Someone was cooking breakfast. Everything felt perfectly right. I continued laying on the bed trying to wake up all the way. I wondered where my mom was. I rose up but continued sitting in the bed. To my surprise, my cousin Tanya walked in. She was six years older than me. I hadn't seen her since our last family reunion a year ago. What was she doing here? I was happy to see my cousin. I was just puzzled.

Confused

I knew my cousin and her mom lived out of town, but I didn't know the name of where they lived. My cousin Tanya put an outfit, a face towel, and a toothbrush on the dresser for me. She told me to get dressed, wash my face, and brush my teeth. As I was getting dressed, the room door crept ajar. I looked at the door to see who was entering. It was my cousin's mom, Dottie. Her mom and my mom shared the same grandmother. They were the children of two sisters. Dottie gave me a hug and said, "Hey, li'l cousin. Go ahead and get yourself together so you can eat something. I cooked breakfast for you." I said, "Where is my mama?" She said, "She went to take care of business."

Boujie Family Members

That was beginning to become the theme of things when my mom was unaccounted for. My sisters began waking up, and my cousin Dottie got them situated also. My cousin Dottie, her daughter, my two sisters, and I went to the table to eat breakfast. When we finished breakfast, I got a chance to explore the rest of the house. It was an apartment like the apartment that we just moved out of. My cousin Tanya had toys in her room. When I saw them, I instantly went toward her toy box. Her room was so organized and clean. I was happy. I knew we were about to play with her toys. She had some pretty cool toys that I'd never seen before. As I began to pull the toys out of the toy box, my cousin Dottie said, "Put those toys back." Her tone changed from how it first sounded when she told me she had breakfast ready. Then I remembered my mom and her sister talking about our out of town family members. They were talking about how boujie the family that lived out of town were. They said they think they are all of that, and they think their kids are better than everyone else.

The Nag

I remembered them mentioning our cousin Dottie's name. As I was putting the toys back in the toy bucket, my mom walked in the door. She walked into the first room I woke up in. She put her purse on the top of the closet in that room. We stayed there at my cousin Dottie's house for six months. Every day that we were there, it got more miserable each day. Our cousin Dottie complained daily. She fussed about everything and anything.

Why the Chaos

I was in the first room that I woke up in on one Sunday afternoon. I heard a bunch of screaming and yelling. I opened the door to the room to see who was yelling and screaming. When I opened the door, I saw that my mom and Dottie were in a screaming match. My cousin Dottie saw that I opened the door. She yelled at me, telling me to get back in there and shut the room door. When I shut the room door, they continued to yell and scream. I couldn't make out what they were saying clearly. Then my mom barged into the room. She told me to get my shoes on. She started putting my sisters' coats and shoes on. Once we were all suited to going outside, my mom picked up the phone that was in the room that we were in. She made a phone call. Thirty minutes later, there was knock on the front door. My cousin answered door, then she called in the back room for my mom. My mom grabbed her purse and our blankets. We all went toward the front door.

At the Front Door

De'Lye was at the front door waiting to help us carry our things out. He helped my mom put all our belongings in the trunk of my mom's car. He drove us around to the backside of the same complex that Dottie stayed in. Once we got parked, a man, who stood five eight with a bald head, came out to help us take our belongings inside of another apartment. Once we got inside the apartment, I saw that the apartment looked just like Dottie's apartment. De'Lye introduced my mom to the man. The man shook my mom's hand and said his name was Mike.

Mike

He told her his wife left him, so he lived alone. He had a three-bed room apartment. Mike took us on a tour of the apartment, showing us where everything was located. We got to the furthest room down the hall. When we got to the room, Mike opened the room door. He said this room was for the girls. Everyone helped tote our things into the room. My mom put our blankets on the bed to make it comfortable for us and then she left out of the room. I was walking toward the kitchen. My mom was in the second room down the hall toward the left. I saw her in the mirror dressing up. De'Lye was sitting on the bed talking to her.

The Turtle Takes the Water

She looked like a superstar. She had so many curls in her hair. Her makeup was perfect. She had on a pretty red dress. I stopped at the room Mike had given to her and De'Lye to live in. I said, "Mama, you look so pretty. Where are you going?" She said, "I am going to see the turtle takes the water." I said, "Huh? Can I go?" She said, "If you go, the turtle will not take the water." I kept trying to picture a turtle taking water. My mom would become a beautiful superstar/model every night at the same time over the next year. Once she was beautified, she and De'Lye would leave. They left at the same time every night at 10:00 p.m. They came back home the same time every morning at 6:00 a.m.

Flowers in the Attic

It got to the point where I hardly saw my mom. My sisters and I spent 75% of our time in that bedroom watching television, coloring, and entertaining each other. One night, I was awakened out of my sleep. I woke up because my whole side of the bed was wet. When I got too cold, I wet the bed. I got out of the bed. I walked down the hallway to my mom and De'Lye's room. When I opened the room door, I saw that they were not in there. Then I walked across the hall from my mom and De'Lye's room to the bathroom. I turned the bathroom light on. I don't know why I thought I would find them in there.

Where's Mama?

Once I turned the bathroom light off, I walked one door down the hallway to the right. That was Mike's room. His door was left ajar. He had a night light on in his room that enabled me to see that no one was in his room. I continued to walk down the hallway. Once I got to the entrance of the living room and where the hallway ended, I saw a man lying on the couch. I could tell by the physique of the person that it was not my mom or De'Lye. Mike was laying on the couch. I walked up to the couch. I tapped him and said, "Mike, do you know where my mama is?" He jumped up, startled. He said, "Oh crap, girl, you scared me." He said, "She is at work." He asked me, "What's wrong?" I started crying. I sobbingly said, "I wet the bed. I need to clean it up."

My Comforter

He hugged me as I sobbed. Mike said, "Don't cry. It was an accident. We will clean it up." Mike grabbed my hand and walked me back to the bedroom where my sisters were. He cut on the light in the closet. He was trying not to wake my sisters. He started looking through our clothes. He found me a long dress to put on and some panties. He got two body towels. Mike walked over to the bed where my sisters were sleeping. He laid the towel over the piss spot. He walked back over to me with my clothes and towel in hand. He said, "See, it's okay. You don't have to cry. We will clean it up tomorrow when your sisters wake up." At that moment, I thought he was the nicest person I ever knew. I cried because I was embarrassed about pissing on myself. He made me feel comfortable and assured. I didn't feel so ashamed.

Bed Wetter

I also cried because when I experienced bed wetting at earlier times, I would get an ass whipping. I was relieved that Mike didn't give me an ass whipping. He was my hero. We proceeded to walk toward the bathroom. He ran my bath water and put some bubbles in the tub. Once the tub was half full, he cut the water off. He told me he was going to place my clothes and towel on the bottom shelf, so I could reach them when I got out of the tub.

Getting Clean

Mike walked out of the bathroom and pulled the door shut behind him. I couldn't wait to get out of those pissy clothes. They were starting to itch. I immediately pulled my clothes off and jumped in the tub. I splashed and played in the bubbles until the bubbles begin to dissipate. I pulled the plug on the drain to let the water out of the tub. I got out of the tub and dried off. I put my dress on, but I could not find my panties. I walked out of the bathroom. I didn't have to ask Mike to get me more panties. I thought, *I'm a big girl. I can get them myself.* When I came out the bathroom, I looked to the right into the living room. Mike was lying on the couch sleep. I went back to the left toward me and my sisters' room. I was going to find me some panties and lay back down on top of the towel that Mike put down for me. I took one step toward our room. Mike's voice startled me. He said, "Where you going?"

A Pissy Mess

"You can't lay on that pissy bed. It's still wet." I said, "I need to get something." He said, "Come here right quick. Let me tell you something." I obeyed. I walked to the couch where he was lying. Mike reached his arms out for me. I leaned into his arms. He picked me up and laid me on top of him on the couch. He hugged me, making me lay flat on top of him. He began telling me how pretty and special I was. Then he said, "One day you are going to make someone a good wife." I lay there quiet while he talked. Then when I tried to rise up, he hugged me again. He said, "Why were you crying when you told me you pissed on yourself." I didn't say anything. I didn't want to relive that. I thought to myself, *He is about to give me a whipping.* Then he said, "It was an accident, right?" I said, "Yes." Then he said, "You think you are going to get in trouble if I tell your mom?" I said, "Yes." He said, "What do you think will happen?" I said, "I'm a get a whipping." He said, "We don't want that."

A Secret

Then he said, "Well, we must make sure this stays our secret." I was relieved. I tried to rise up again. He hugged me tighter. I began to feel uncomfortable. Mike's hand slid down to my midsection. He pulled me tighter to him at the mid area. I felt his middle area. It didn't feel like it felt when he laid me on top of him at first. It felt like a hard brick or something. I didn't understand what was going on why was it so hard. I thought he had something in his pants that wasn't supposed to be there. He grabbed my bottom tighter and started gyrating his hips around. *What in the world was he doing*, I thought. After he gyrated for about five minutes or so, he rose up on the couch. He picked me up and stood on both feet. Mike swung me over his shoulders to his back.

Piggy Back Ride

He was giving me a piggy back ride. Mike walked to the front door of the apartment and put the top lock on the already locked door. He walked me to his bedroom. He said, "You can sleep in here with me because you wet your bed." Mike laid me down on the bed. He walked away from the bed to his room door. He shut the door and locked it. Mike spread the blanket on the bed. The blanket covered me. Mike crawled into the bed next to me. He asked me if I was okay. I didn't say anything. I didn't know what to say. He said, "I want to give you a back massage. Have you ever had one?" I still didn't say anything. He continued talking and asking questions. Every time he asked me a question, he had the answer for me for each question that he asked me.

Twenty-One Questions

I didn't understand what was going on. During questioning, he started rubbing my legs. He told me to turn over. He was going to rub my back. I remembered I didn't have any panties on. I was ashamed to get naked in front of any one that was not my mom or sisters. I was afraid and confused. This couldn't be something that was right. Then I thought, *But this is Mike. We live with him. I know him. He's not going to tell my mom. He is the nicest person I know.* Feeling ashamed, I said, "You can't rub my back because I need to get some panties on."

Twenty-One Answers

He told me it was okay. He said he would just ignore it. Then he told me his eyes could put imaginary panties on me. He rose my dress up slowly. I thought he was going to turn me over to rub my back. That was what he said, but he didn't. He went down to my inner thigh and started licking and kissing. It felt gross. I didn't like it. I didn't like it when my sister slobbered on me in their sleep. I didn't like playing in the mud or dirt. I didn't like anything that resembled slime, boogers, or spit. I was grossed out. He began to moan and make noises. I didn't understand why. The noises frightened me. He asked me if I like it. I didn't say anything. Again, he answered the question for me. He said, "Yes, you like it. You know it's good." It sounded like one of my little sisters when they were eating a bowl of spaghetti or Jell-O. My stomach felt sick. I felt like I wanted to throw up. I almost wished I could've thrown up on his head. Maybe then he would stop.

Rescue Me

I heard the bathroom toilet flush. He heard it also because he jumped up faster than comic book hero THE FLASH. He pulled my dress back down. He said, "I think somebody is here." Then he said, "I'm going to make sure your mom doesn't find out you pissed on yourself. Remember, it's our secret." I said, "Okay." Then he said, "Stand right here by the back of the door. I'm going to come back and get you." He walked out the room for a minute or two, then I heard my sister crying. She was asking for me and my mama. When I heard her crying, I rushed out of Mike's room. I ran to my sister. Mike had her by her hand. He was trying to lead her back to our room. He said he was going to put her back to sleep. I grabbed her hand from Mike.

Lock the Door

I took her back into our room and locked the door. Mike knocked on the door and asked was she okay. I said, "Yes, I am going to help her go back to sleep. We are okay." I lay in the bed next to my two sisters trying not to lay on the piss spot. I fell asleep next to my sisters. I was awakened by a knock on the door. It was my mom. I heard her say "Open this door. Don't lock the doors around here." I ran to the door to let my mom in. I hugged her so tight. Then my sisters walked over, and we all hugged. I began to cry. She said, "Girl, what is wrong with you?" Mike walked into the room. He said, "I gave them some Sweet tea last night. They accidentally wasted it. Let me change these covers." He pulled all the covers off the bed. As he was pulling the covers off the bed, De'Lye called my mom to come to him. He was in his and my mom's room. I tried to follow her, but she stopped me from following her and said, "I will be back."

He Is a Saint

When my mom walked out of the room, Mike continued cleaning the bed and changing the linens. He asked me if I was hungry. I didn't say anything. He answered his own question the same way he did the night before. He said, "Sure you all are hungry. You haven't had anything to eat. I went to the store and got you some ice cream. Do you want one after you eat?" I knew I loved ice cream, so I said yes. Two months had passed. Every night when I got sleepy, I locked the door. I felt an obligation to protect myself and my sisters. Every day, Mike had something new that he purchased for me. He purchased dolls, coloring books, snacks, and ice cream. He would always give the gift to me in front of my mom. I heard her telling De'Lye, "Mike is so nice to the girls. He is a God send." I thought to myself, *TUH.*

Post Sexual Abuse

The third month came. I wet the bed more than ever before. Instead of going out of the room or trying to get help to change the covers, I pulled all the covers off the bed. Like clockwork, Mike changed the covers and cleaned the bed every morning. Four months post sexual abuse, I felt myself growing up faster than the average children around me. My eyes were losing innocents. When I watched television, I picked up on the sexual content in things. I understood sexual adult humor that I didn't understand before. I became fearful of everything, and I didn't trust anyone. I didn't care to play with dolls and coloring books any more. I was thinking about running away and getting my own place. How was I going to do that? I was just a kid, I often thought.

Family Outing

De'Lye's mom stayed around the corner from Mike's. Everywhere in Waco was around the corner from each other. You could walk from the north side to the south side. Each walk would take thirty minutes at the max. My mom put some clothes out for my sisters and I to put on. She seemed a nervous wreck. She wanted us to be perfect. She groomed us and cleaned us to exceptional perfection. The last time I remember looking as nice as we did that day was... wait I couldn't remember a day or a time. My mom and her boyfriend got really fancy also. They were good at making first impressions. We looked like a nice family that was going on an outing. Once we all got settled and dressed, we started to walk. I didn't understand why we were walking, and we had a car. I asked my mom, "Why are we walking?" She said, "We need to get exercise. We taking a family walk. It is a beautiful day outside. We are going to meet De'Lye's mom. Don't talk unless she talks to you. Don't ask any questions and y'all better be on your best behavior." I said, "Yes, ma'am." I could always tell when something was very important to her. Her focus changed. Usually her attention was scattered. She always seemed like there was always something on her mind, or if there was some other place she rather be than right there in the moment, doing whatever we were doing.

Dusty Little Town

When we left Mike's apartment, we walked northbound from the apartment complex. We got to the edge of the complex where a street was paved. The street ran east and west. We crossed the street and continued walking north. When we made it across the street, the street changed. It was all dirt and rock. There were trees and bushes that surrounded the dirt and rock road. It looked like we were headed to the forest or something. We continued to walk. We made it midway down the dirt road. I noticed the traffic flow was getting heavier. I saw a brown car. I believe it was a Regal. When we stayed in Austin, I remember seeing the letters on the car, so I knew this kind of car. The car passed us up three times. My mom and her boyfriend were busy conversing about things to say when we got in front of his family. I don't think they noticed the car.

When the car drove passed us again for the fourth time, I said, "Mama, I saw that car pass us four times. They must be lost." My mom and her boyfriend looked at the car in a dead stare. De'Lye said to my mom, "As soon as the car makes it to the stop sign, we are going to run through these woods on the left." As he was saying that, he was picking up my youngest sister. My mom said, "Ty, we are going to race. So when De'Lye says go, we are all going to run into the woods. Don't stop running until I tell you to stop." I was excited. I loved running. I could run fast. My second born sister was always my shadow. Whatever I did, she did also. My mom knew all she had to do was give me instruction, and my sister was going to follow the same instructions. As if it was her my mom was talking to. They didn't take their eyes off the car. They watched the car drive down the street slowly. Once the car made it to the stop sign, the car turned right. De'Lye quickly said, "GO!"

Track Star

I took off running as fast as I could. No matter how fast I ran, I couldn't outrun De'Lye. I saw him in my peripheral. He was coming up on me to the left. He was carrying my youngest sister. He still managed to leave me by some yards. When I looked to my right, my mom was scooping my second born sister up in her arms. She was running also. While running, she said, "Run faster, Ty. Faster." I ran faster. We ran hard for five minutes. I was getting tired. Running no longer seemed like a race anymore. It felt like we were running from something. I kept seeing my mom looking back. *What was she looking for?* I thought. *Did it have something to do with the Regal I spotted?* We were hidden somewhere in the woods. There were a lot of trails and trees. These woods led to the backyards of the neighborhood houses. My mom's boyfriend knew the area all too well. I thought we were lost, but he knew exactly where we were.

Deep in the Woods

Once we were deep into the woods, we came to an acre of space. The space had a bob wire fence around it. We walked around the back of the fence, then we turned right and walked alongside the side of the fence. We got to a part of the fence that had a lock and key on the fence. Dogs started to bark. I was afraid of dogs. When I heard those dogs, I shot off like a bullet running the opposite way. I made it to the back end of the gate. While in my stride, I heard my mom call my name. She said, "TY, DON'T RUN. THEY ARE ALL CHAINED UP!" I thought I was going to piss on myself. My mom and her boyfriend were laughing. They laughed uncontrollably. I mean they had tears in their eyes, holding their guts laughing. I couldn't appreciate that because I didn't see what was so funny. I journeyed back to where my mom and De'Lye were, standing at the side of the gate. When I was almost back to where I heard the dogs barking, I saw De'Lye's face change. He was trying to contain his laughter.

Who Let the Dogs Out?

I watched him dig into his right pocket and then he dug into his left pocket. He was looking for something in his pockets. He pulled his hands out of his left pocket. Then he opened his hand. In his hand, he held a small key. When he pulled the key out of his pocket, he inserted the key into the lock on the gate. The gate opened. All I could hear were dogs barking When we got in the gate, I looked to the right where I heard all the barking. I wanted to make sure the dogs were chained up. I saw four dog houses spread out toward the center back of the yard. We were standing six yards away from where the dog houses were placed. When I looked to the left, six yards left I saw a door. The door was up a set of six stairs that where at the back a building that looked like an old monumental house. When I looked behind me, De'Lye was still holding my sister in his arms while putting the lock back on the fence. I heard a noise. It was on my left where I just saw the door and the stairs. When I looked to follow the sound of the noise, I heard big voice say, "GAL, what you doing back there? Where ya folks at?"

Trespassing

I was astonished. I didn't know what to say. I couldn't see his face. I just saw that he was tall. He was standing in the doorway, but there was a screen on the door. He couldn't see De'Lye or my mom because they were out of view of the door opening. De'Lye quickly walked over to where I was standing. He said, "Pops, it's me." The back-screen door came open. The man that De'Lye called Pops was standing there with a shot gun in his hand. Once he saw that we were no threat, Pops went back into the doorway. We followed De'Lye up the stairs to the door. De'Lye held the door open for us to enter. When we made it through the door, I found that we were in the kitchen. This was the back door to the house. My sense of smell was intrigued. Something was cooking in the oven in that kitchen. When I walked into the kitchen, four feet away was a refrigerator. That was the first thing I saw. It was in alignment of the door opening. When I looked to my left about seven feet away, there was a heavy-set woman in the kitchen. She was sitting in a chair next to the oven. The sink was to the back left of her, and the oven was to the back right of her. I didn't know what to expect. She had a mean unexpecting look on her face.

Mrs. Love

The look looked as if she was saying who in the hell are these people in my house. To my surprise she was the sweetest person I had met in that town since we got there. She reached her arms out to me. She said, "Hey, beautiful, come over here and give me a hug. I'm going to be your new grandma!" De'Lye said, "Mama, that is Ty." Then he introduced my mom and my two little sisters. His mom gave all of us big hugs. She said, "The food is almost done. I hope y'all brought y'all appetites 'cause I'm gone fatten y'all up. Y'all are a part of the family now." Then she said, "Now y'all gone in there and meet the rest of y'all family." His mom's name was Mrs. Love. She invited us to her family barbecue. I guess we were being accepted as family. I could never forget the first time I met Mrs. Love. She was the true definition of love. We followed De'Lye out of the kitchen.

When we stepped out of the kitchen, there was a room across the hall from the kitchen. We walked to the left down the hallway. We passed up a bathroom on the left and a bed room on the right. We continued walking down the hall until we got to another bed room on the left. There were kids and teenagers in this room playing video games, watching TV, and listening to music. De'Lye stopped in this room and introduced us to all the people who were in that room. Once we were done in that room, we went back into the hallway and proceeded to walk toward a big wide-open space. This was the living room. All the grownups were in the living room drinking beer and watching football games on TV. De'Lye introduced us to all the adults also. I didn't care about being introduced to all the adults. I was ready to go play with the kids. Something else we hadn't done much of since we moved to this town. I went to the room with kids. We played and had a good time. One of my new cousins had a Walkman. I thought this was the coolest thing ever. The only time I saw one of these things was on TV. Now I was getting to use one. I was already having fun. I found a space that was not being occupied. It was on a little couch up against the wall.

Vibration

I was listening to the Walkman for fifteen minutes before I felt a big vibration against the wall. When I reacted to the vibration, I looked up to see that everyone in the room was reacting to it. I instantly pulled the headphones off my head. I heard commotion. I heard the voices of two adult males. They were arguing. I recognized De'Lye's voice. He was one amongst the quarrel. I didn't understand what they were arguing about. I thought we were all having fun. I walked to the doorway to see what was going on. As soon as I walked to the doorway of the room, I saw De'Lye flying across the room. He was going head first. His feet were in the air like he was going to save the day. All he needed was a cape. His head hit the window. I looked at the window where his head hit. The window did not crack. I saw several cars parked in the yard. De'Lye landed on the couch after his head hit the window. I looked to see how he was able to fly. I saw De'Lye's older brother. He looked like De'Lye, but his body frame was taller and wider. His eyes were big like he was shocked also. He stood in a stance like he was waiting to see what De'Lye was going to do. De'Lye had a look on his face as if he wanted to cry.

Here Comes Mama

His mom, Mrs. Love, rushed out of the kitchen. My mom was following behind her. Mrs. Love said, "What the hell is going on in here.?" When De'Lye saw my mom and his mom, he ran passed them in the hallway. I thought to myself, *Where is he going?* De'Lye's brother sat back down in his chair. Their mom said, "I said what the hell is going on?" De'Lye's brother said, "Nothing, Mama. Don't worry about it." His mama was about to ask again. Before she could get the question out of her mouth, De'Lye rushed past her and my mom. He pushed my mom out of the way and charged his brother. De'Lye had a knife in his hand. He put the knife to his brother's neck. Mrs. Love started screaming hysterically, "NO! NO! NO! NO! Somebody get him." She was terrified. De'Lye had a look in his face like he was ready to kill his brother. De'Lye's older brother was in fear for his life. He sat their stiff being careful not to make any sudden movement. I couldn't believe it.

My life, Your Entertainment

The things I was starting to see or had happened to me, I thought only happened on TV. TV was now becoming my reality. De'Lye's dad ran into the first bedroom across from the kitchen. I heard the shotgun cock. He rushed back into the living room. He pointed his shotgun toward De'Lye and his brother. Pops said, "I'm gone kill both of you motherfuckers today. Y'all ain't gone give my wife no damn heart attack." De'Lye eased the knife off his brother neck. I took the knife back into the kitchen. The other family members sat there like it was a normal thing. Pops went back into the room across the kitchen. He put his gun up. I watched him walk back into the living room. He sat down in his chair and continued drinking his beer. Mrs. Love and my mom walked back into the kitchen. De'Lye returned to the living room. His brother whom he just put a knife to his neck handed him a beer. They proceeded to watch the game like nothing had happened.

Where They Do That At?

I was on edge. What in the trailer park projects just happened? My thoughts were interrupted by the sweet voice of Mrs. love. She said, "The food is ready. Everybody come eat." Everyone piled into the kitchen. It was fifteen to twenty family members in the kitchen. We were waiting to eat. Pops came in and told everyone to grab hands around the table. We all grabbed hands. Pops blessed the food. Mrs. Love said, "Kids eat first. Once we get the kids' plates fixed, everyone else can eat." The adults got all the kids' plates made. We went into the room closest to the living room and ate. The food was so good. They had all kind of meats that they barbecued, cakes, pies, and all the sides. They even barbecued a whole pig on a stick. Now that was something very new to me. I thought to myself, *It's not so bad here.* I was actually having fun. After a while, people started leaving.

A Rat That Looked Like a Cat

I felt myself getting sleepy. I told my mom I was getting sleepy. She asked Mrs. Love was there somewhere that I could lie down. Mrs. Love gave me a blanket. She told me to go lie in the room across from the kitchen. I went to lie down. I fell fast asleep. It felt like I was sleep for forty-five minutes to an hour, but when I woke up, the TV was on the news and said it was 10:30 p.m. I knew that it was 7:00 p.m. when I fell asleep because they were saying that was the time that the final game was going to come on. My sisters were lying next to me. I rose my head looking straight into the kitchen. I saw a rat as big as a baby cat ran across the kitchen floor. Then my mom and De'Lye walked in. My mom was very fancy again. She looked like a celebrity as she did every night. My mom said, "I didn't know you were awoke. Try to go back to sleep." I lay back down. I heard my mom's boyfriend say, "I don't want her to stay here if she is not sleeping because my mom must go to work in the morning." My mom said, "You just gone have to keep her then." He said, "All right. We will take her with us." I was happy to go to work with my mom and De'Lye. I was finally going to get to see how the turtle took the water. Beside that rat cat had me terrified. I left with my mom and her boyfriend that night. While I was sleeping, I figured my mom and De'Lye went to Mike's apartment complex to get the car, and because they changed into their fancy clothes.

Pimping and Prostitution

Once we were in the car, my mom asked De'Lye why he and his brother were fighting. He said, "Because he thought I was being disrespectful to our parents." My mom said, "How?" De'Lye said, "He thinks that you are one of my jobs." My mom said, "A worker?" He said, "Yeah." My mom got quiet. I don't think she liked the answer he gave her. There was a brief moment of silence. She said, "How many bitches have you had done this? So, am I your woman or you pimping me?" He said, "Watch your mouth. Ty in the car." There was another moment of silence. Then the questions started coming. "How many of them have you taken to meet your parents?" He said, "I don't want to get into all of that. We will talk about it later. Let's just make this money tonight." My mom said, "Cover your ears, Ty." I put both of my fingers in my ears. I couldn't hear anything at first, but then she started yelling. I heard her say, "IM OUT HERE SELLING MY PUSSY MAKING ALL THIS MONEY! Motherfucker, I don't need you to manage my shit! I manage my own shit! You got me fucked up! I wouldn't never be in this situation if I wouldn't have met your sorry ass." Then she said, "I knew I should've stayed in Austin." He said, "I love you. Shut yo stupid ass up! You are not like the other ones. You are going to be my wife someday."

She's Calmed

Something about that statement calmed her. De'Lye pulled up in a convenience store parking lot. My mom got out and started walking. She got two blocks up the street, and a car picked her up. I watched my mom drive off in the car. I asked De'Lye where my mama was going. He said, "Don't worry about it. Do you want me to buy you something out of this store?" I said yes. He said, "It is too late for you to be out there. I need you to stay in the car. Tell me what it is that you want from inside the store, and I will get it for you." I told him I want some chips, candy, and a drink. De'Lye told me to lock the doors behind him. I climbed over to the front seat from the back. I locked the doors when De'Lye got out of the car. Then I climbed back into the back seat. I got myself positioned comfortably in the back seat.

Déjà Vu

I saw the brown Regal from earlier that day. The Regal continued to circle the parking lot just as it circled the block earlier. I wanted to know who was in this car. Did my mom and De'Lye know these people or this car? Why did they circle the perimeter? I wanted to get out of the car and tell De'Lye that car is there again. When I looked through the window of the store, I saw De'Lye at the cash register paying for my purchases. The Regal parked on the left side of our car. Once the car was parked, I saw the driver side of the car door open. A man that stood maybe the same height as De'Lye or a little taller stepped out of the car. He shut the car door behind him. He walked toward the entrance of the store and stood on the side of the door. He planted his back up against the wall. Then he propped his right foot up and planted it on the wall that he posted his back on. De'Lye was coming out of the store. De'Lye pushed the convenience store door open. He began walking toward the car. He didn't see the guy standing to the left side of the door. As soon as he stepped off the curb, I started yelling, "De'Lye, watch out he's going to get you." De'Lye saw my facial expression and my gestures. He had a confused look on his face like he was trying to understand my excitement.

The Barrel of a Gun

I was yelling, "Look behind you." De'Lye turned around just in time enough to see the barrel of a gun. The strange man had a gun pointed to De'Lye's head. A second guy got out of the passenger side of the car. He ran to his partner. The first assailant hit De'Lye over the head with the gun. His partner kicked him in the back. I felt numb. I wanted to cry and scream, but I couldn't see any means to do that. *What would it help*, I thought. I watched the two men beat De'Lye for twelve long minutes. When the guys were done beating him, the driver with the gun leaned down to De'Lye where he was lying on the ground. He pointed the gun to his head. I couldn't make out what he was saying because the windows were still up. The passenger ran back to the car. The driver followed. They jumped in the car and sped away. I could see the convenience store clerk on the phone. I assumed he was calling the cops. I got out of the car. I ran to De'Lye. I was trying to help him get up. He was bleeding everywhere. When I went to his aide, he yelled at me. He told me to get my butt back in the car. I ran back to the car.

Limping and Bleeding

He finally made it to the car, limping and bleeding. He got in the car, and we drove around. After driving for thirty minutes, we pulled up behind a white Chevy Impala at a red light. When the light turned green, we followed the car through the light. The car pulled up at a drive-through chicken place. The chicken place was closed. It was one o'clock in the morning. My mom got out of the Impala. I didn't understand how she got in that car because when she left us, she was getting in another car. My mom came to our car. When she saw De'Lye, she panicked. She started asking him questions. He murmured out the name Rick. My mom instantly knew whom he was speaking of because she didn't ask any more questions. My mom helped De'Lye over to the passenger seat. She got in the driver's seat and drove away. We drove back to Mrs. Love's house. My mom ran in the house to get my little sisters. Our final stop that night was Mike's apartment.

Grab My Purse

When we pulled up at his house, I instantly became nauseated. My mom went to Mike's front door while we sat in the car. When she came back outside, he came outside with her. My mom helped De'Lye get in the house. Once she made sure he was in the house safe, she came back to get my youngest sister. Mike carried my second younger sister. She told me to grab her purse and carry it in. I did as I was told. As I was grabbing my mom's purse off the floor of the front seat, Mike was locking the car doors. He walked around to the passenger side where I was getting my mom's purse out of the front seat. He had my sister on his left shoulder. He extended his right hand for me to grab. I didn't want to hold his hand. He kept his hand extended as if he was ignoring my hesitation. I grabbed his hand. He walked my sisters and me into the house. My youngest sister was already in the bed asleep. Mike put my second younger sister in the bed next to her.

Monster Under My Bed

My mom was in the room with De'Lye helping him. Mike picked me up and hugged me extremely tight. He told me that he had missed me. I was scared. He asked me if I'd missed him too. I didn't, but I said yeah. I was pushing him away trying to get down. He ignored just as he did that night. I was once afraid of a lot of things like the dark and monsters under my bed, but Mike was the monster under my bed. I tried to push away again, and he ignored the push. He kissed me on my lips saying he was so glad that I was back. Then he continued kissing me all over my face. I closed my eyes real tight, and I prayed. I said, "God, save me from the monster." Just as I said that, I heard my mom. Room door cracked open. Mike positioned his kisses as if they were more appropriate. My mom came out of the room. She got some warm towels and a bucket of water. She took all those things back into her room, but before closing the room door, she told me to go get in the bed and lie down. She said, "It is too late for you to still be up." I was never been so happy to go to sleep. I said, "Yes, ma'am."

Shut the Door and Lock It

Mike put me down and walked away from our room door. I went to my mom's door and gave her purse. After I gave her purse, I walked back into our room, shut the door and locked it. I was relieved. Over the next two weeks, my mom continued her routine at night. De'Lye stayed home with us at Mike's house. I think he needed to recuperate. He was banged up pretty bad. His body needed some time to heal. That weekend while my sisters was napping, Mike asked my mom if he could take me to the park and to get some ice cream. When he asked her, I instantly felt sick. My mom said, "Yes. That would be fine." Mike told me to go find my shoes and put them on, and we would go. I went in the bedroom. I lay down. I was supposed to be looking for my shoes. I didn't want to find them. I lay on the bed and got under the covers. I closed my eyes real tight, and I started praying, "God, save me from the monster." Before I could think another thought, I fell asleep fast.

Back to Work

My mom woke me up telling me to go use the bathroom so I wouldn't wet the bed. I rushed to the bathroom. She was dressed like a celebrity again. This time, De'Lye was dressed up also. When I was done using the bathroom, I rushed back to our room. This routine continued for two more weeks. The monster had no access to me anymore. My mom and De'Lye were dressing flashier than ever before. One day, I walked passed my mom's room door. The door was cracked, and I was peeping in. I saw my mom empty her purse. The purse was a gray backpack purse. It had Cs all over it. When she emptied the bag, the money covered the entirety of the bed. De'Lye pulled out four more duffle bags full of money. They both looked like celebrities. They dressed liked this all the time now. De'Lye began to wear more jewelry—several neck chains, rings, and bracelets. They even bought a new car.

Traveling Grace

I went to sleep one night and woke up in the back seat of the new car. We drove for so long, I fell asleep again. When I woke up again, I was lying on a couch. This place was not familiar to me. I didn't know where we were. My two sisters were lying on the couch with me. I walked around the place looking for my mom. When I got to the bathroom area, I walked into the bathroom. I turned the bathroom light on. Inside the bathroom was another door that led to a second bathroom that was right next to the first bathroom. I went through the door of the second bathroom. When I walked out of the door of the second bathroom, I was in a bedroom. My mom and De'Lye were lying in the bed asleep. I walked back to the living room area where my sisters and I were sleeping on the couch. There was a glass sliding door that led to the side of a huge backyard. I checked to make sure the door was locked on the sliding door. Then I walked to the right of me where I saw a front door. I checked the locks on the front door. I looked out the window that was next to the door. I saw the new car and the old one parked in the driveway. There was also a moving truck parked next to the curb by the house.

Breakfast at Home

After I locked the front door, I lay back down. I couldn't sleep. I stayed awake until my mom and sisters started waking up. My mom woke up in a very happy mood. She woke up making us breakfast. I hadn't had her breakfast in a while. Mike was always making breakfast. My mom asked me if I wanted to help her make breakfast. I said, "Yes, ma'am." She cut the television on in the living room and sat my sisters down in front of the television. They watched cartoons. My mom and I began to make breakfast. She asked me how I liked our new place. I said, "I like it a lot." I wanted to know who else would be living with us in the new place. I asked her, "Does Mike live here also?" She said, "No. Just me, you, your sisters, and De'Lye." I felt relieved. Then I said, "Where are we? Are we still in De'Lye's hometown?" She said, "No, we are back in our own hometown."

I Missed My Austin Family

I asked her if we could visit our cousins and my dad. She said yes. After we finished eating breakfast and getting dressed, my mom called my dad on the phone. I wanted to see him so bad. When we left town, I was unable to see him or talk to him for two years. A couple of hours later, my dad came to pick me up. He took me to his mom's house. I hung out with his sister and brother. They were still teenagers. When it was time to fall asleep, I lay in the bed with my grandmother. We talked a long time. I told her about how fancy my mom and De'Lye had become. I told her how they left every night at the same time. I may have mentioned a few things about Mike, but I didn't remember everything I told her because I was falling asleep.

Uproar

The next morning, the whole house was in an uproar. I didn't know what was going on. My dad was on the phone arguing with my mom. I heard my dad say, "So that hoe dude pimping you and you prostituting?" I didn't know what he was talking about, or why he was saying that to my mom. What did pimping and prostituting mean? I was curious to know. I thought my mom and De'Lye were working. They were making a lot of money. I did know that when you have a job, you go to work and make money. I thought what they were doing was called going to see the turtle takes the water. Wait a minute, I did remember my mom asking De'Lye if he was pimping her during an argument. Wait a minute, was this what they were speaking of? I stayed at my dad's mom's house for a week. My mom called every day. My dad said, "I will let her come home when I beat the fuck out of the piece of shit of a man you have." Then he hung up in her face. I heard my dad talking to his mom. He said, "This pussy of a man got my daughter's mom prostituting for him. He might be trying to pimp the kids out too. Hell, I don't know. I tell you one thing, if I find out somebody has fucked over my daughter or her sisters, I'm busting they mama ass for letting it happen." Then I heard my uncle (my dad's little brother) say, "I'm going to kill that motherfucker." My grandma said, "Y'all call down. I have been hearing a lot of things through different people, but we must find out facts." Forty-five minutes after my dad hung up in my mom's face, the cops were knocking at the door. My mom was with the cops. The cops told my dad that his visitation time was over, and that he needed to surrender me to me my mom.

Going Back to Court

My dad told my mom he was going to take her back to court. I could not understand what just happened. When I got in the car, my mom and De'Lye were speaking discreetly. They were talking about my dad. She said, "He says he is going to take me back to court." Then she said, "I will talk to you about it later." De'Lye drove to Jam Burgers burger joint. I thought he was going to go through the drive-through. Instead, he put the car in reverse and parked at the last parking section closest to the exit. De'Lye walked around the building toward the back of the burger joint. I watched him walk until I no longer saw him anymore.

The Rat Race

My mom, my two little sisters, and I were sitting in the car. My mom was snapping her fingers to a song that was playing on the radio. My sisters and I were sitting in the back seat laughing at our mom. Our giggles and chuckles were interrupted when my mom bolted out the words "WHAT THE FUCK!" I looked up to see what she was reacting to. I saw a mob of men running from a mile away. They were headed in the direction of our car. The closer they got, I noticed that De'Lye was leading the pack. He ran faster than I ever saw him run. He had a look on his face that looked like he saw a ghost. He looked like he was in fear for his life. The mob of men was maybe two yards behind him. I could tell he got an early start, or he was just a super-fast runner. At first, I thought they were with him, but the closer they got, I realized they were chasing him.

The Getaway

My mom quickly flung open the passenger door and jumped from the passenger side to the driver side of the car. She turned the keys that were already left in the ignition. My eyes stayed fixated on the mob of men. "Why were they chasing him?" I wondered. When De'Lye reached the car, he jumped in fast slamming and locking the door behind him. My mom put the car in drive, and we sped away like we were on a high-speed chase. I looked back in the back window at the mob of angry men. They were becoming more distant the further we drove. I noticed something, all of the guys that were chasing De'Lye had familiar faces. I recognized all of them.

Everything Is My Fault

De'Lye turned around to the back seat and yelled, "THIS IS YOUR FAULT!" He raised his hand to strike me, but my mom grabbed his hand. She looked him in the eyes with a dead set stare and yelled, "DON'T!" De'Lye said, "You need to whip her ass. She told them that I touched her the wrong way." My mom asked me if I did say that. I said, "No, I didn't say that." My mom asked, "Has anyone ever did something to you that you didn't want done to you besides when you've gotten a spanking?" I got quiet. I didn't say anything. I was afraid that if I told on Mike he would tell my mom that I pissed on myself that night. Then she said, "Well has someone?" I tried to speak, but my voice cracked when I spoke, then I started crying uncontrollably. My mom pulled over in a grocery store parking lot. Once she parked the car, she turned around and looked me in in the eye. Tears were beginning to form in her eyes. She was anticipating what I was about to say.

Get Out of the Car

She opened her car door. Then she got out of the car. Once she was out of the car, she opened the door to the back seat on the side where I was sitting. She told me to get out of the car. She bent down to my height and started hugging me. She said, "It's okay. You are not going to get in trouble, and I am not mad at you. You need to tell me if someone has hurt you." I told her what happened that night with Mike. She cried and asked why I didn't tell her before. I told her how scared I was, and when I tried to tell her, she was always gone. She looked at me in thought like she was thinking back on something. When she rose to her full height, a car swooped up quickly.

Kidnapping

They swooped up on De'Lye's side of the car. Some men jumped out of the car. The pulled De'Lye out of the front seat of the car. The men shoved De'Lye in the back seat of their car. They drove away. Once again, I noticed all the guys. They were my uncle's friends. My mom called my dad. She told him what I had told her. I figured my dad asked for Mike's name and address because my mom was telling my dad all of Mike's information. He was furious. He told her he was going to kill him. My mom asked my dad if he had something to do with the guys taking De'Lye. My dad said, "That dude out of there too." My mom said, "Why? I just told you who hurt your daughter." My dad became enraged. I could hear him yelling through the car phone.

You Didn't Know?

He said, "Your dumb ass so naïve and blind you the only one that doesn't know who molested your sister's daughter." I could hear my dad screaming through the phone. He said, "Why you quiet? You didn't know?" My mom said, "No I didn't know." Then my dad said, "What is that town full of fucking Chesters?" My mom hung up in his face. When my mom got off the phone, she asked me if De'Lye had ever touched me. I said, "No, ma'am. But I did see Elijah pull his ding dong out of his pants."

Police Are Contacted

My mom said, "You don't have to worry about Mike anymore. Your dad is headed to Waco." I remembered earlier, my dad said he was going to kill someone if he finds out someone did something to hurt me or my sisters. He was going to kill them. When my mom told me he was headed to Waco, I knew something was going to happen. My mom called the authorities. When she finished talking to me, she informed them of the abuse that occurred to me. The authorities said they contacted Waco police. The Waco police were going to pick Mike up. Four hours later the phone rang. My dad was calling my mom from the Waco police station.

Beat Inches from Living

He and my uncle beat Mike so bad that he was hospitalized. Unfortunately, the authorities in Waco were called to a disturbance at Mike's place. My dad and uncle beat him five inches from his life. Shockingly, my mom drove to Waco and posted my dad and uncles bond. Mike was in the hospital handcuffed to a hospital bed. Once he was released from the hospital, Waco police picked him up. He confessed to all that he did to me and was given a prison sentence. My dad and uncle's charges were dropped from aggravated assault to disorderly conduct. A year had gone by. I don't know what happened to De'Lye because we didn't hear from him again. Our lives were getting as close to normal that they could get. My mom got a call. When she got off the phone, she walked me into my room. She said Mike was raped and killed in prison. I don't know why I wasn't satisfied by this. I felt a sadness for Mike. I didn't expect to hear that. At the same time, when I heard he got killed, my sense of paranoia subsided a little. I felt like somebody killed the monster under my bed. My childhood made me a very cautious adult. I am a better parent to my children because of all the things that I endured. I have better understanding and communication. I can empathize with similarities and provide advice and support. At times I wish I could take a magic wand to wipe away my past, I realize my past has shaped and molded me. I am enjoying and appreciating everything I am coming to be. I am strong. I survived, and I persevered.

He Loves Me to Death

Operating Table

I see flashing lights. Next, I see flashes of my life, then I'm travel-ing through the speed of light. I know that I'm not dead because I feel excruciating pain from my toes to my head. What is going on? Something went wrong. I can't remember anything. There is damage to my brain. My vision isn't clear. I can't see, but I can hear. The nurse said to the doctor, "Can we save her life?" The doctor said, "I'm not feeling confident. She was shot twice, one in the leg and one in the head." I couldn't remember my name and who or what did this to me? My spirit is floating over my body. I am lying on an operating table hooked up to tubes and cables. The machines giving me oxygen to breathe, but I can't take or catch a breath. I went to clinch my chest as if I was having a heart attack, but my hand went straight though my back. What's going on? What went wrong? Now something's coming back—more flashes of my life. I see a silhouette of a man standing over me. He's crying and begging please. Once the crying ceased, he started dragging me by my feet. I'm in and out, out and in.

A Broken Start

I came from a broken home. No parent just grandparent that were not always capable. My grandparent took in their five grandchildren. There was my sister Elijah, who was my cousin. She was the oldest of the five. Next there was me, TyshAnn. I was the second oldest. After me was Kymara, Elijah's birth sister. Then there was Kelise and Felise, my two-birth sister. They were twins. Elijah and Kymara's birth mom passed away when they were five and six years old. Our mom went to prison shortly after Elijah and Kymara's mom passed away. The night my mom went to jail, I remember being in the back of her friend's car. His name was Womack. For some reason, we called him Uncle Womack. I don't know how he was our uncle because he wasn't my grandmother son. The year was 1987. I was six years old. Kelise, Felise and I were sleeping. I woke up to flashing lights and loud bull horns saying "PUT YOUR HANDS BEHIND YOUR BACK!"

Excessive Force

I was startled by this. I didn't know what was going on. I rose my head slowly to look out of the back mirror, but the trunk of the car was raised up. I couldn't see anything. I was very inquiring, analytical, and observing. At such a young age, I had to figure it out. I climbed over from the back seat to the front passenger seat of the car. I barely put my head out the window. I didn't want anyone to see me. I saw Womack and an officer. The two of them were standing in front of the officer's car. The officer was kicking Womack's feet apart in a separating motion. Then the officer slammed Womack's face on the hood of the car. He was using excessive force. I didn't understand why the officer was treating him that way. The officer put the handcuffs on Womack. The officer pulled Womack off the hood and walked him to back door of his squad. I saw the back car door open. The officer threw him in the back seat and slammed the back door. He slammed the back door as if he was locking him up and throwing away the key.

Mama Under Arrest

My eyes glanced up to the left side of the patrol car that had Womack in it. I saw another patrol car emerging from around the first car. This patrol car had my mom in it. I remember praying that the officer did not treat my mom the way the first officer treated Womack. The officer in the second patrol car that had my mom in it pulled up on the side of Womack's car. I thought to myself, *He saw me. Now he's going to kill me! Lord Jesus, please don't let him kill me.* I forgot my two sisters were still asleep in the back seat.

Do What Mama Says

The officer didn't kill us. That was the first time I ever really felt like prayer really worked. He pulled up parallel to the car my sisters and I were in. He pulled up close enough for my mom to talk to me. The officer rolled my mom's window down. She said, "I'm about to go to jail. Do you remember Grandma's number?" I said, "Yes ma'am." She said, "Okay, that's good. Somebody gone come get y'all and bring y'all to the jail. Don't be scared. When you get to the jail call grandma. Tell her to come get y'all before Child Protective Services does." I didn't know who Child Protective Services were, but I knew she trusted me to do exactly what she told me to do. A squad car with a woman officer and a man officer pulled up. The man officer stayed in the car. The woman officer got out of the squad car and begin to converse with the officer that had my mom in the car.

My Mama Is Leaving

After they were done conversing, the second officer got back in his patrol car. He drove off with my mom in the car. I was afraid, but I knew my mom was counting on me. The female officer of the third car walked over to the car where we were in. She informed me that we were going to leave with her. She said she was going to take us to the police department so we could be safe. I woke my sister Kelise up. I helped her out of the car. My sister and I stood by the car door. The female officer lifted my sister Felise from the back seat. She grabbed my hand after shutting De'Lye's car door. I grabbed my sister, Kelise's hand tighter. Hands conjoined, we walked to the third squad car. The female officer opened the back door of the squad car. She placed Felise in the back seat and motioned for Kelise and me to get in. She closed the door behind us when we were safely in the car. I watched the female officer walk around to the passenger seat of the car. She got in the car. I took my eyes off the female officer for a second to realize the first squad car that Womack was being detained in was still sitting there. I noticed the squad car because it was to the left of the third squad. I kept seeing its light in my peripheral. I was curious to know what they were doing. Why hadn't they left yet.

At the Police Station

The female officer and the male officer got us to the police station just as the female officer said. The female officer motioned for me and my sister Kelise to walk up a flight of stair. The officer continued to carry Felise. *How could she sleep through all of this?* I thought. When we made it to the second floor, I saw my mom being escorted out of a room and into an open space area. The opened space area was being occupied by other inmates. The inmates were sitting in blue chairs, but they were all linked from chain to person. When I saw my mom, I attempted to run to her. The female officer grabbed my hand and said, "No, no, sweetie. You can't do that." My mom looked at me and didn't say anything. I continued to walk with the female officer and my sister. She took us into a room. The room had a phone, a desk, and a computer.

Be Strong

The room was cold. I said to the officer, "My sister is cold." I kept trying to be strong. I didn't want her to know I was the one who really was cold. The officer said, "I will see what I can do." The entrance didn't have a door on it. It was just walls and an entrance. The female officer stood by the entrance of this room. She kept looking out like she was looking for someone. Moments later, I heard her greeting someone. I heard her say, "I'm going to go find some accommodating items for the children." I couldn't see who she was talking to because the person hadn't walked close enough to the entrance, but I knew it was a woman. The other female officer entered the entrance way along with a male officer and a nurse. They were being nice to us. I still was afraid. I told the nurse that I need to call my grandma. The nurse allowed me to call.

Call Grandma

I dialed my grandma's number. The first time I called, she didn't pick up. I knew that if she didn't pick up, the department of Child Protective Services were going to come get us. I knew that with a long name like that and from the severity of my mom's tone, they couldn't be any good for us. Thinking back on what my mom said and how she said it, I began to panic. I started dialing the number over and over. I was praying, "God, please let Grandma pick up. Please, Grandma, pick up." The nurse hung the phone up before I could attempt to dial for the tenth time. I said, "Why did you do that? I need to talk to my grandma or somebody bad are gone come get us!" I could no longer hold back how strong I was trying to be. I cried like a newborn baby, wanting a bottle.

Cried Out

The nurse hugged me and consoled me. She said, "It's okay, honey. Your grandmother is probably sleeping like the rest of the world. It is three o'clock in the morning. We will try again in about three or four hours." I sniffled and cried. I felt like I failed my mama. Now somebody who wasn't supposed to get us were going to get us. All because I couldn't get in touch with Grandma. I heard the male officer tell the second female officer that they would wait three or four hours to call Child Protective Services. The female officer looked very empathetic. When I looked up, I looked into her eyes. I was awaiting her response to what the male officer just said. She looked just as doubtful as I did. I cried harder. I continued praying in my head, *Help us, God.* The nurse continued to hold and console me. I was just a kid. I never saw any of the TV shows or books I read end up this way. The other female officer and the male officer were trying to entertain my sisters. They continued coloring on blank paper with pencils and pens. I'm so glad they were easily entertained. When I felt I was all cried out, I sighed.

Sense of Peace

I started feeling warm. I felt a sense of warm goodness come over me. The first female officer made it back. She had PB&J sandwiches, apples, oranges, apple juice, and milk. She brought three stuffed bears, three sleeping cots, and three blankets. The first female officer gave my sisters their food. They ate it graciously. The nurse and the female officers lay them down on their cots and put blankets on them. They fell fast asleep. With all the chaos, I forgot that I was hungry. After the nurse cleaned me up, I ate my food and lay down on my cot. I went to sleep. That was the most peaceful sleep I had in a long time. I was so drained and worried. I just wanted a break from it all. I was hoping I would go to sleep and wake up to find that I was just having a bad dream. I slept hard for maybe two hours. I woke up to a voice saying, "TyshAnn, wake up." I opened my eyes to see the silhouette of a dark shadow and a curly head of hair. It was Uncle Womack's brother, Uncle Art. He was there to pick my sisters and me up from the police department. I didn't know if my mom or his brother told him to come get us. I was just relieved that it wasn't Child Protective Services. When we made it to Grandma's house, Womack's brother knocked on the door. My great-grandmother answered the door to let us in. My great-grandmother took my sisters and me to the bedroom. I lay down in the bed closest to the door, and I slept.

Grandma's Grief

About four hours into my sleep, I heard another voice saying, "Ty, wake up." It was my grandmother. She was just making it in the house. I later found out that she was not home when we arrived. When she woke me up, she asked, "Where is your mama?" I said, "In jail, Grandma." She said, "Oh no!" She asked, "Do you know why?" I said, "No, ma'am." She said, "Okay. Go back to sleep." I heard her voice crack when she said oh no. She sounded as if she wanted to cry. I heard her telling my great-grandmother and my grandfather that she was worried about my mom. She said she needed to make a visit to the jail to see for herself. I heard my grandfather ask her, "So did Womack go to jail too?" My grandmother said, "He passed away before he could make it to the jail. Rumor has it that the feds were looking for Womack. He been smuggling drugs across the border and over state lines for the past three years now." My grandpa said, "Wow." Grandma said, "I could've told you that everyone in East Austin knew. How do you think he was able to open all those night clubs?" My grandma new everything that happened in the streets because she would shoot pool, and she did some illegal gambling herself.

Street-Savvy Grandma

My grandpa was green to the new streets because he was no longer hanging out in the streets. He went to work and came home trying to a live an honest life. Grandma went on to say, "Yeah, he was working with crooked cops. Those cops kept tampering with the evidence." Grandpa said, "He probably got caught with some drugs on him. He may have been using Nae as a scapegoat." Grandma said "Yes, if he had drugs in the trunk of the car. I don't think Nae knew they were in there. I hope not 'cause that sure would be stupid to put herself in that kind of situation with her children." Grandpa said, "Did they identify the arresting officer?" Grandma said, "Yes. So far everything points to him being one of the bad ones, but we won't know everything for sure until the investigation is over."

"He may have crossed the wrong crooked cop," said Grandpa.

"Ain't no telling. I'm just glad that I'm not burying Nae Nae," said Grandma. She continued saying, "I feel really bad for his family. I hope they can get some answers."

Eavesdropping

Grandma ended the discussion saying, "I will tell the children later." I was listening, but I was thinking in my head. I didn't care to know. I felt like Womack was the reason for my mom being in this situation, and because she was in this situation so were we. My mom and men equaled a disaster. I don't know why or how she could fall weak to these men in her life. I saw my mom as such a strong woman. Every time she dealt with a man, our entire lives changed for the worse. So for me, Womack was one less thing to worry about. I couldn't go right back to sleep after that. I was worried that Grandma sounded worried. I rose up to put the cover back on my feet. I realized I was lying in the bed with my sister Elijah, who was actually my cousin. I looked across the room by the window, and there was another bed. My sister Kelise and Felise were sleeping on one end of the bed, and my sister Kymara, who was actually my cousin, was sleeping on the other end of the bed. Reality began to sink in. I started having a three-day-old flashback. My mom was crying and screaming. She fainted. Several people were standing around her, trying to lift her off the ground. Kymara was running, and her dad was chasing after her. Elijah was crying uncontrollably and inconsolably. My grandmother was in the same state of being that Elijah was in. We were in a big church building.

A Tisket, a Casket

All the seats and pews were filled to capacity. Everyone was crying. I observed and watched everyone's response. I felt invisible. It felt like everyone in the room was in motion. I was the only one in a stand still. I fixated my eyes in front of me. I was standing at the start of a long aisle. My eyes adjusted again seeming to magnify x's two on what was in front of me. It was a zoom in on what was on the opposite end of the aisle. There was a brown oversized rectangular box. The lid of the box was open. There was a person inside. I couldn't get close to see the person inside, but I knew it was my only aunt on my mom's side. My mom's only sibling, Elijah and Kymara's mom. My grandmother's firstborn daughter.

The New Reality

I heard yelling and screaming. I opened my eyes and jumped up. I looked over to my left; there was a digital alarm clock that read 1:36 p.m. My sisters were no longer lying in the beds. I guess I had fallen back to sleep. My soul was shaking. I was breathing heavily, trying to figure out what the commotion was about. I walked out of the room to figure out where everyone was and what was going on. My grandma and grandpa were fussing at each other. Apparently, my grandmother hadn't been home in two days. My grandfather was worried about her and didn't understand where she'd been. My mom and her sister had children young. Our grandparents weren't traditional aged elderly grandparents. They were mid aged. This went on for ten long minutes. Amid the argument, Grandma said, "I'm going to the store to get something to cook." We waited on Grandma's return. Grandma did not return for a whole week. While she was gone, my great-grandmother went to live with one of her other children. She was way too old to be bothered with everything that came with five bad kids. My grandfather continued to be the supervising adult. Grandpa and Grandma worked better when they were working together. When Grandma did not come back, all the girls and I had to take care of ourselves. We looked out and cared for each other. I was the nurturer. I organized and created meals with the little we had. Grandpa continued to go to work every day.

The Sixth Day

Grandma came back on the sixth day. I wanted to fuss at her myself. But I was just a kid. The adults often told the kids that worried or asked too many questions to stay in a kid's place. Besides we were just all so happy to see her. Disappearing acts became a habit of Grandma's over the course of the next six years. When grandma disappeared, we stuck to the routine. We took care of each other. At times Grandpa seemed unbothered about grandma being gone. Those were good days. Then there would come bad days. Everything we did started getting on Grandpa's nerves. He was a calm man, but when he snapped, he beat the hell out of all of us. Small things would set him off.

Slapped for Popcorn

Grandpa went into the kitchen, put his popcorn over the stove top, and popped it. He loved popcorn. Sometimes he would bring the kernels home from work. Once the popcorn was done, he put it in a big bowl for sharing but did not want to share his popcorn. We were all hungry. There was no food in the house for us to eat. We thought he brought it home to share. That was not what he was thinking. Elijah put her hands in his bowl to grab some popcorn, and he slapped her a flip. The next fit of rage was directed toward me. One day, I came out of the bedroom. My grandfather put his hand up to me like he was going to give me a high five and pushed me back. Using the deepest meanest tone of voice, he said, "GO BACK IN THERE AND DO NOT COME BACK OUT!" He hardly ever raised his voice. I was shocked and scared. When I looked into his eyes, I no longer saw him. I was so scared. I turned myself around and went back into the bedroom. I shut the bedroom door.

Kymara Is Brave

My sisters were looking just as shocked as I was. Two of my sisters were sitting on the couch in the room that we all shared, and two were sitting on the bed. I heard the door come back open. My grandpa came in. He rushed to me and grabbed me by the back of my neck. I looked down, and my feet were lifted off the ground. I was in midair. I heard a thud. My back and head pained. He'd thrown me into the wall. I was just glad I didn't go through the wall. I didn't cry. I just sat there. I was in shock. Random slaps and chokes happened frequently. They happened mostly when Grandma disappeared.

Jail Time

I started to think a slap or choke from time to time was normal. I used to tell my sisters at least he didn't leave us. When I rose to see everyone's faces, all my sisters were looking back at me. Then I watched everyone's eyes go from one sister to another. Everyone was awaiting the next person's reaction. My sister Kymara jumped off the couch. She stood by the room door and started crying. Kymara charged out of the room. As if she wanted to kill our grandpa. I pulled myself together to follow behind Kymara. The rest of my sisters followed me. Kymara barged into the living room area where our grandpa was sitting. She pointed her index finger at Grandpa as if she was pointing blame. She screamed at my grandpa. I was shocked because she was the shy and introverted one. She yelled, "YOU ARE GOING TO JAIL!" She called our grandpa by his government name. I thought, *WHOA she is brave.* I never saw her stand up to any one like that not even for herself. Kymara's crying and screaming started a domino effect. We were all standing there with Kymara crying.

A Trusting, Praying Family

She ran out the door to the neighbor's house, and we all ran behind her. That night we slept at the neighbor's house. They were a spiritual church going family. We trusted them. The mother was just preparing dinner plates. When we came over, the dad asked us if we were hungry and if we had eaten. We hardly ever had any food at home, so of course we were hungry. When the dad asked us if we were hungry, we all said yes at the same time. We were all on one accord. For the first time, we all sat down at the table as a family. The father told us to grab hands, and that he was going to say GRACE. My sister Kelise said, "What is GRACE?" The father of the family said, "Grace is when we give honor to God." Felise said, "Honor to God?" The father said, "Yes we are going to thank God for providing this meal." He told us to bow our heads and close our eyes. The father begins to pray, "Our Father who art in heaven, Hallowed be thy name. Thy kingdom come. Thy will be done on earth as it is in heaven. Give us this day our daily bread and forgive us for our debts as we forgive our debtors. Lead us not into temptation but deliver us from evil. For thine is the kingdom and the glory forever. Lord God, thank you for this food, the hands that prepared them, and this day we get to share as a big family." After he finished praying, I felt a sense of peace. This feeling always came after a solid prayer. That was how I knew God was real. That was the second time in my life that I encountered that spiritual warmth that gave me a sense of peace. It was like the whole room was at calm peace. I looked around the table as food was being passed and conversations were being had. Everyone at the table was smiling and laughing. We all forget the moments that transpired to this moment.

After Dinner

My sister and I were not strangers to helping cook and clean because we often did it for each other. I told the wife, "Don't worry. We will do all the cleaning." She said, "No, sugar, it's all right. I love cleaning and cooking for my love ones." I asked her, "So you love us?" She said, "Yes, honey!" I said, "Honey? Sugar? Why do you talk like that?" She chuckled then she said, "That's love talk, sugar!" She said, "Now you go in there with your sisters. They are in the guest bedroom." I walked out of the kitchen into a hallway that extended left. The guest bedroom was the first door on the right. They had an entertainment system with a TV, a home stereo, and Nintendo game system connected. There was a computer desk with a computer on it and two long sofas. The dad was unfolding the couches out. They turned into two beds. He gathered blankets and pillows for us once we all were lying down. The wife came in and kissed us all on the cheek. She told us to get rest, and we would sort things out in the morning. She turned the light out as she exited the room. That night we all stayed up talking. We talked about how good the food was and how nice they were being to us. Elijah said, "Why can't we just live over here with them." I said, "For real. At least we would have food to eat." Kymara said, "Did y'all see the Nintendo game system they have? I wish we could play it." She changed the subject. I think she just wanted to forget about our realities for the time being. So, we all followed suit of the subject change.

Give Us this Day Our Daily Bread

We were having such a good time. We were excited about the moment. I had to keep reminding everyone to keep their voices down. I remembered what the father said at dinner about grace. I remembered the sense of peace that came over me every time I prayed. I saw enough TV shows to know how to pray. I prayed whenever I was in trouble or really needed God. But this family showed us how to say GRACE. I thought maybe we should thank God. So, I told my sisters what I was thinking, and we all agreed. It would be a good idea to give thanks to God for the best night we had in a long time. We took turns from the oldest to the youngest giving thanks and saying our grace. By the time Felise said the final prayer, the whole room was warm but cool at the same time. I felt a different sense of peace. I felt an overwhelming peace that showed me at that moment, and that time was where we were all supposed to be praying, asking, and giving thanks for the rest of our lives no matter who or what. I don't think any of us had a care or worry for that moment. We were all love and smiles. It seemed as if we all became instantly calmed. Before you know it, we were all sound asleep.

Here She Comes

About six o'clock in the morning, the roosters were crowing. It wasn't quite daylight yet. I heard the doorbell ring. I woke up easily. I was half awake anyways. I looked around the room. All my sisters were sleeping. I heard the door crack then open. When I looked toward the door, it was the wife. She peeped her head in the doorway. She said, "Wake up, my loves. Your grandmother is here." We were always happy to see Grandma when she came back home, but we were not ready to go back to our real lives. We were enjoying this new life. Everyone started waking up. We put our shoes and socks on in a dragging manner.

Granny Is Home

I could tell, we all were feeling the same thing. We all were so happy to see Grandma again. Every time she came back, it was as if we started all over again. Everything wasn't perfect, but they were okay. No one ever wanted to believe that she would disappear again, so we just made the best of each moment. Four months went by, Grandma was still hanging around. Our grandpa was happy, so were we. There was no violence, no mood swings, or arguments. Grandma was here to stay this time. We went to school, excited to get back home to a normal functioning life with Grandma and Grandpa. When we walked in the door, Kelise and Felise headed to the kitchen. Elijah, Kymara, and I went to Grandma's room ready to tell her about our day. Grandma was nowhere to be found. We waited around talking and figuring. At 6:00 p.m., Grandpa walked in the door. Elijah said, "Hey, Grandpa, where is Grandma?" He didn't say anything. He walked into his room and shut the door. We all looked at each other because we already knew that nothing had changed. This continued over the course of the next two years.

Growing Up

In the summer of 1995, we moved in to a more urban neighborhood. Grandma's health started taking a toll over on her. She began to stay at home more. By this time, Kymara, Elijah, and I were young teenagers. Guys started taking notice to the beautiful young women we were becoming. Elijah, Kymara, and I were walking through the neighborhood to the neighborhood candy store. Halfway to the candy store, a white Cadillac pulled over to the side of the curb. We all continued walking. The Cadillac drove slowly alongside of us as we walked. I looked to Kymara and said, "Do you know that car?" She said, "No." Elijah said, "Just keep walking. It's enough of us in a group to make sure we are okay." The driver's side car window started rolling down. A guy put his head out the window.

Meet and Greet

"Excuse me, will you come talk to me for a second." We looked at each other from girl to girl not knowing whom he was speaking to. He parked his car, and we all continued walking. This guy opened his car door and got out of the car. He walked to the left side of the group of girls. He grabbed my hand. I snatched it back. He said, "Hi. I didn't mean any harm. I just want to get to know you. My name is Q." I was still reluctant to tell him my name. I wasn't having relationships outside of us girls. We taught each other to always be cautious. Then he said, "Do you have a name?" I said yes but still not telling him. He continued to walk with us, engaging in conversations with the girls and me. He left his car half a block down the street to walk with us. We made it to the candy lady's house. I knocked on the door of the candy house. The owner came to take our orders. Once everyone ordered their sodas, pickles, candies, and chips, Q ordered a soda. He told all the girls, "I got it." Q pulled out a big wad of money and paid the candy lady for all the items that we purchased. The four other girls that we were walking with, Elijah, Kymara, and I started whispering in my ear. They were telling me who he was.

Gold Diggers

They lived in that very neighborhood from when they were small. We were new to the area. One of the girls said, "Girl, you better talk to him. He got that money." I blew it off. That wasn't of my caliber. We grew up without money our entire lives. Money was not one of the things we wished for as kids. Once he paid for everyone's goodies, it's like they were sold. They started walking ahead of Q and me. They were letting him have alone time with me. He asked, "So are you gone tell me your name?" I said, "My name is TyshAnn." He said, "Okay. Now I have something to go on." He took a genuine interest in me. He wanted to know all my likes, dislikes, what made me laugh, smile, and cry. He wanted to know my pet peeves and everything. At this time, there never was a self-evaluation done of myself. The only thing I ever wanted all my life was my mom, food, and Grandma. I never thought about the things that I like or didn't. Our aunts bought us donation clothes from the local thrift stores when we were younger. We often got the hand-me-downs from other family members. We ate whatever was available. We didn't grow up with many choices. All those questions he asked me, I'd never thought about until then.

The Ride of Our Lives

He asked me if I wanted to take a ride with him. I said, "Only if my sisters can go too." He said, "Cool." When we made it back to his car, my sisters were waiting like guard dogs. I don't know where the other girls disappeared to. Elijah had her own thing going on, so she told to Kymara to ride with us. Elijah asked Q if he had a pen in his car. Q gave Elijah a pen. She wrote the license plate number of his car on the palm of her hand. Everything that we'd been through made us all cautious and protective of each other. Q walked around to the passenger side door. He opened the door for me and allowed me to sit in the seat. He shut the door behind me. Kymara opened the back passenger door. She got in, and he made it to the driver side and got in the car.

On Average

He drove us around to see what the average day looked like with him. He asked us if we were hungry, and of course we always were. There was hardly ever any food at our house. The first place he took us was to a steak and lobster restaurant. I ate like I was starving that day. I saw potatoes and steak. We never had lobster and steak before. We had chicken a lot of times but not steak and lobster. He was so happy that we were so gracious and easily pleased. After eating, I was happier than I'd ever been. We were full for the first time in a very long time. He asked us what type of music we liked. Neither of us said anything. He pulled out a long case with a bunch of cassette tapes in it. "Brass Monkey" by the Beastie Boys popped on. When the music turned on, the bass went boom. It startled me at first. I think it startled Kymara also because when I looked in the back seat at her, she jumped, and we both started laughing. We drove around town. Every place or house he went to, we didn't stay long. He knew everyone all over the town. Q started introducing me to everyone that we met as his li'l mama. I didn't know what that was. It was the first time I heard it. I just stayed quiet and went along with the ride.

He's a Generous Man

It was getting late. I knew our grandma would be looking for us. He drove us home. Q parked in the parking lot that was adjacent to our house. Kymara got out of the car and went into the house. Q told me he enjoyed being around me and wanted to hang out again. He gave me his home number and told me to call him. I got out the car and went into the house. Thank God Grandma was already in her room asleep with the door shut. She hadn't even noticed that we were gone. We were full and happy. Over the next ten months, Q and I hung out. He continued taking me and sometimes my sisters to the finest restaurants. He was very generous with money and gifts. Every time he would see me, he'd come bearing gifts. I enjoyed the times I would have when I was with him. He adored me also. I went for a ride with Q. Today the routine was different. Q took me to meet his family. He introduced me to his family as his girlfriend. In my mind, I thought to myself, *I am his girlfriend.* I was happy to be his girlfriend. Every time I saw him, nothing but good came from our times together. I thought, *He must really love me because he makes sure I eat.* Now he's introducing me to his family as his girlfriend. Yes, I am his girlfriend. Another year passed, I was sure I was in love with him. Life was looking better than it's ever looked.

Lunch Time

Every Friday, Q would bring me lunch to school. We ate lunch in the courtyard of the school. After eating lunch with him, I would return to class. He encouraged it. By this year, I was glowing in full effect. My face was prettier. My physique was in fine form. I'd come into my most beautiful and attractive physical. I was dressing nicer and eating better. A lot of the guys at my high school were into my sisters and me. We had the ugly duckling turned into swan syndrome. On this Friday, I was supposed to meet Q at the front of the school at 12:30 p.m. I went to the front of the school as scheduled. My lunch was from 12:30 p.m. until 1:30 p.m.

No Worries

When he did not arrive, I wondered, but I didn't worry much. I figured he just got busy. I told myself that I would call him later once I got out of school. I rushed to the cafeteria with twelve minutes remaining to grab a bite to eat for lunch. I walked into the cafeteria. A group of jocks were sitting at the table whistling and taunting as I walked by. I ignored them. I walked into the lunch line. As I was grabbing my lunch tray, I felt someone's hands around my waist from the back. I turned to see who it was. One of the jocks followed me into the line. I put my tray down on the counter and pushed him away from me. He leaned towards me once again, grabbing and pulling me close to him. He had both of his arms around my arms. His hands were locked around my back. I couldn't pull away.

You Don't Want No Problems

I heard a voice say, "Hey, playboy, you DO NOT WANT THEM problems." It was Q. I was relieved to hear his voice. The jock let me go instantly. He joined his friends and walked off. Q purchased my lunch and apologized for being late. I got a quick hot pocket lunch on the go. I returned to class. When the second school bell rung, school was out. I walked to the side of the school building. The school buses parked on that side. The school bus that we rode was called the butterfly. For some reason, the bus driver that drove the butterfly was always late. This caused our bus to always be the eighth bus to the back of the line. I walked to the back of the line. My sisters were already aboard the bus. I stepped onto the first step of the bus. I heard a horn blowing. I looked to my right into the side view mirror of the butterfly. I saw Q's car parked in the back of the bus. He was waving at me, motioning for me to come to his car. Everybody on the bus turned around to see who was blowing at the bus. I stepped of the last step. I was all smiles walking toward his car. I was so happy to see him. I opened the car door and sat in the seat. He reminded me to put my seat belt on. We followed behind the school buses until we were out of the parking lot of the school. The school buses went to the right, and we went to the left.

Something Is Not Right

Q kept looking in his rearview mirror as if he were looking for something to come behind us. Q asked me how my day was. I went to explain my day as usual. He continued driving as I talked. He pulled up in an empty parking lot where there were constructions being done. The workers had already gone for the day. I wondered what we were doing at this empty lot. Q then asked me, "Who was that nigga hugging all on you when I came to your school?" He took his seat belt off to turn sideways to look at me in the face as I spoke. I said, "This stupid football player. They are always…" Before I could get the words out of my mouth, his hands were around my neck.

He Tried to Kill Me

His arm's length was at full extension. My head was up against the window of the car. I was gasping for air. I couldn't catch my breath. He was saying something to me, but I couldn't hear him. I saw his facial expression and his eyes, and it didn't look like the Q I knew. He looked possessed. It reminded me of the same face I'd saw in my grandpa earlier in life. He continued talking while squeezing and pushing tighter. I went out of consciousness. Although I was out for a minute or two, it seemed like I was out for an hour or so. I saw my auntie, Elijah and Kymara's mom. She was so angelic. There were beautiful white lights surrounding her. She had two bodyguard figures hovering with her. They were also angelic. She told me I was going to be okay this time. She told me to go home and stay away from Q. When I regained consciousness, Q was crying while trying to wake me up. When he saw that I was okay, he started hugging and kissing me. I was confused. I didn't understand why this happened. I didn't know who this person was or what happened to him in between after school and now. He was crying and apologizing. I was crying and confused.

Can You Take Me Home?

I just wanted to go home. I told him, "Can you please take me home." He said, "Yes. Are you okay?" I didn't say anything. I was still trying to figure out what just happened. On the way home, he stopped at a shopping mall. He bought me an outfit shoes, a necklace, and a ring. Then went to the very first restaurant he took Kymara and me to. I ate and got full. It seemed as if nothing ever happened after that. Q took me home. I avoided him for four days. He called my grandma and grandpa's house phone. When my sisters answered, he asked to speak to me. They would hang up in his face. When my grandma and grandma would answer, he would hang up instantly.

Anonymous Calls

Q started calling from anonymous and private phone numbers. I decided to answer one of the calls. When he heard my voice, I could hear the instant excitement in his tone. I was almost happy to hear his voice also. The more he talked, the more I missed him. I couldn't understand why I was feeling conflicted in my feelings. He promised me that he would never hurt me again. He said his life had been so miserable without me in it. He said these four days seemed like an eternity in hell. He asked if he could take me out to eat. He said that we would talk over dinner. I was hesitant at first but something in me wanted to know why he did this or what happened to him. He sounded so sincerely remorseful. Besides he was the first and only person that I knew to ever show a genuine interest in me.

Getting Back to Us

He really loved me was what I thought. Then I went on to add... at least he fed me. At least he bought us clothes and things we never had. I didn't realize it, but there I was making the same excuses for him that I made for Grandpa. I agreed to let him take me out to eat as long as my sisters could come. He agreed to let my sisters come along. This time all five of us went. He took all of us shopping and out to eat. I think, by the time we were full, everyone forgot why we were mad at him. This continued for the next two weeks. Things were beginning to go back to normal. I found myself liking him again. The fourth week came. I began to let down my defenses. We were almost back to the way we started.

Surprises, Surprises

By Friday, Q came to eat lunch with me as usual. On this day, we didn't eat lunch at the school courtyard. We went to my favorite steak and lobster restaurant. After eating, he took me to a shopping center. He told me to sit in the car, and he would return. I watched him run into the jewelry store. My lips were feeling dry. I remembered I needed a ChapStick. I took the keys out of the ignition and locked the car doors as I got out of the car. My thought was to run into the Dollar store while he was in the jewelry store. I was going through the checkout line. Two guys were standing behind me. I saw them before. I couldn't quite remember them, but I knew I'd seen them before. The taller guy asked me if my name was Ty. I said yes, but I didn't understand how he knew my nickname. I didn't know them or their names. The short one said, "We saw you with Q." Then he went on to explain.

Jealousy

Q walked in the store. Q said, "Hey, baby. I was looking for you." He walked up to me and hugged me as if he wanted everyone to know I was with him. Once he noticed who the guys where, he spoke to them. He gave them handshakes. I told him I would return to the car while he talked with them. He said, "Okay." I went to the car. About five minutes later, he came back to the car. We drove away. He was quiet. He wasn't full of energy as he was earlier. I wanted to ask him was everything okay, but I didn't. He drove, and I rode. We pulled up at a condominium. I thought he was going in and then out like usual. He told me to get out. He wanted to show me something. I got out of the car a little hesitant because his mood was different. I didn't know what to expect. He walked to the door and opened it with the key. He said, "I got this place for us. Once you graduate, this belongs to you."

Not My Thoughts

I hadn't thought about moving in my own house, yet I was still in high school. Then he said, "That's not it." He had a bag in his hand. He reached into it pulling out a box. He said, "I love you, Ty. I know that you are still in school, and I am five years older than you, but no one gives me what you do." Then he fell to his knees and asked me to marry him. I'd never thought about marriage. All I knew was that I was his li'l mama and then his girlfriend. I was cool when he introduced me as his li'l mama. I really loved it when he introduced me as his girlfriend although he never conversed with me about those changes. I was cool going along with it. Now he was saying this condominium was mine. He was asking me to marry him. I wasn't ready for that part.

Am I Dead?

That didn't sit right with me. He asked me so many things about myself, but he forgot to include me in on the matters of his heart and desires. I started thinking about college and graduating. I started thinking about leaving my sisters. These things were running through my mind. He was down on one knee awaiting my answer. I grabbed both of his hand to help him up off the floor. Once he got up on both feet, he said, "I guess you don't want to marry me." His mood changed again. I saw it change. He walked to the back room. I wanted to run out the door, but I thought I could reason with him. He said he loved me. He said he would never hurt me again, so maybe he wouldn't. He came back out of the back room. I was standing by the front door. He said, "What you gone leave?" I said, "No, I think we should talk." He said, "Talk about what you already said you don't want me." I said, "No, I didn't say that." He said, "You know what they say. You can't take anything with you when you die." Then he laughed and said, "Shit. I'm taking my woman with me when I go." He pulled a gun out his back pocket. I turned around to reach for the door. I heard a loud sound that was deafening. I fell to the floor. I heard another shot that was louder than the first. Then I could no longer see. I went out of consciousness. I saw bright lights.

Operating Table

I see flashing lights. Next, I see flashes of my life, then I'm traveling through the speed of light. I know that I'm not dead because I feel excruciating pain from my toes to my head. What is going on? Something went wrong. I can't remember anything. There is damage to my brain. My vision isn't clear. I can't see, but I can hear. The nurse said to the doctor. "Can we save her life?" The doctor said, "I'm not feeling confident. She was shot twice. One in the leg and one in the head." I couldn't remember my name. Who or what did this to me. My spirit is floating over my body. I am lying on an operating table hooked up to tubes and cables. The machines giving me oxygen to breathe, but I can't catch a breath. I went to clinch my chest as if I was having a heart attack, but my hand went straight though my back. What's going on? What went wrong? Now somethings coming back—more flashes of my life. I see a silhouette of a man standing over me. He's crying and begging please. Once the crying ceased, he started dragging me by my feet. I'm in and out, out and in. It was my aunt again. My aunt wasn't smiling. She looked very sad. She told me not to be scared. She would be there with me the whole way.

I Am a Spirit

I'm a hovering spirit. I see my grandma and grandpa walk in the hospital room together with my sisters. I couldn't hear anything, but I could see. A flat line went across the screen. The nurses and doctors were no longer administering help. My sisters were all crying and screaming. Grandma had a blank stare with a scared look on her face. Grandpa was holding her up while shaking his head. I hovered close to the hospital bed. I couldn't believe this was me. I lay down on my body. I thought if I conjoined my spirit back to my body, I could live. I looked to the sky. I asked, "Lord, why? Why is this happening." I had so many questions, but I already knew why this was happening. I was just trying to prolong death.

Pay Attention to the Signs

I dismissed all the signs. I wasn't blind. I saw the change of moods, the overly jealous streaks, the wads of money. With each gift, I placed my concerns in the back of my mind. I knew better. My aunt told me to leave when he choked me until I couldn't see. I was convicted. I saw what I done wrong. I knew why I was about to die. I stopped thinking and started repenting. I asked God to forgive me for my sins. I became accepting to God's will for my life. Once I calmed my mind, God calmed my soul. My auntie said, "Take a deep breath and just let go." I'd drifted from my earthly conscious to limbo.

Rigor Mortis Sets In

Everything went from being extremely bright to pitch black. I could hear again. I heard the heart monitor beep and then I heard Kymara scream, "Grandpa, somebody go get the doctor. She is not dead. The machine is beeping. She is coming back. Help us. Please, God, bring my sister back!" I tried to open my eyes, but I could not see. I was declared dead for three earthly minutes that seemed like hours in limbo. I made a full recovery. Q was incarcerated. He thought he killed me. He called the emergency system. He confessed to shooting me and said he was going to kill himself, but the authorities closed in on him, and he was apprehended. God showed me his face. He showed me my place. He descended over my world and gave me another chance. When my life flashed over me, I saw my mom and the situations she went through with men. I never understood how she could fall weak to these type of men when she was such a strong woman. God allowed my life to show and answer the question I asked about my mom. She attracted that type because she enjoyed the perks that came with the fast life. Q was older than me and faster in life than I was, but I was attracted to that in a sense. I knew it wouldn't turn out good for me in the end. I knew that those kinds of things don't ever last long. I see it all the time. I was able to give others instruction about the same incidents. My sisters and I grew up talking about these types of situations and how to avoid them. Once we get into the real world, we must put in to action what we know. Sometimes the task becomes a major tested temptation. When we are looking in the face of what's right to do and what feels right to do, we often choose what feels right ignoring what is right. I don't want an earthly mate that will love me to death because that is not love. The devil will not trick me anymore. Going forward with my new life, I will choose to do what's right and not feel right. I will face the world fully armored. God goes in front of me first. I will follow my first mind and my conscience because it is spirit led. He truly loves me because he died for me. Now I live for him. The devil is a defeated foe. He will not trick me anymore.

Never-Ending Love

I felt a never-ending love that sustained my grace. He fixed every broken part of me and made me whole. I knew my worth because I knew he was everything, and it was he that made me. I learned to protect my spirit. I paid attention to people and their behaviors more. I was given better wisdom and insight on individual characteristics. I came alive after I died. I am no longer just existing. I know that life is precious. I asked God to use me. Through me, God gives hope to the hopeless and help to the helpless. I am a sister, a friend, a mother to the motherless. I give peace and rest to the restless. Everywhere I go, I allow people to meet the ultimate love that created me and live in me. I never intended for the unfortunate events of my life to happen, but something good came out of all the misfortunes. I am currently living my life in purpose, but it didn't happen on purpose. For where I'm headed, I found nothing to be worthless. When put in to perspective, it was all worth it.

Drug Related

Victimized

I was maybe five to six steps to the left of JT and the assailant. When I looked to the right of JT, my son Jacob was six or seven steps to his right. My heart shook. I forgot he'd followed his dad into the living area. When my eyes settled at Jacob's face, Jacob was crying and praying. I couldn't hear anything that was coming out of his mouth, but I could read his lips. He had both hands in front of him compressed together. He was saying, "God, please help us." Then he looked at me with his hands in a prayer saying, "Mama, please help us." That moment appeared to be going in slow motion as if it had been chopped and screwed.

Survival Instincts

When I looked at his face, my instinct to survive kicked in. I ran into the kitchen. The sink was full of dirty dishes. I was looking for a knife. I couldn't find one. It seemed like everything was moving so fast. I didn't have any time to have an emotion. My thinking and movement were quick. It's as if I turned into a robot. I couldn't hear anything. Everything I could see was in a shade of red. I opened the dishwasher. I saw a small steak knife. Without thought, I rushed back into the living room area. The only thing I saw was an oversized black-white shadow with a red target on it. By this time, he was telling, "JT, STAND THE FUCK UP. GIVE ME ALL THE WEED AND ALL THE MONEY!" JT was leading the assailant to his mom's bedroom. His mom's bedroom was on the opposite side of the house. When she had her house built, she got the mother-in-law floor plan. The assailant didn't see me as a threat. He felt remorseful when he looked into my eyes.

Unsuspected

I don't think the assailant expected the children and me to be there. When I saw that JT and the assailant were in JT's mom's room, Jerome was walking from the den area into the living room. Jacob was still standing in the same place by the front door in the living room. I quickly gathered my two sons. I rushed them out the back door. Outside the back door was a porch that was fenced in with a wooden gate. I bent down to Jacob's level. I said, "Baby, don't come back in this house no matter what." A part of me wanted to take my children and run the opposite way. Then I thought to myself, *What if the assailant has accomplices? What if someone is waiting outside of the front door?* My mind went blank again. I was still in survival mode. I rushed back into the house from the back porch. As I was rushing back into the house, I heard JT's voice. He was yelling my name. He said, "I GOT HIM! I GOT HIM! COME BUST THIS NIGGA OVER HIS HEAD WITH SOMETHING."

Growth

In the summer of 1995, we moved in to a more urban neighborhood. Guys started taking notice to the beautiful young woman I was becoming. My sisters and I were walking through the neighborhood to the neighborhood candy store. Halfway to the candy store, a white Cadillac pulled over to the side of the curb. We all continued walking. The Cadillac drove slowly alongside of us as we walked. I looked to my sister Kymara and said, "Do you know that car?" She said, "No." My sister Elijah said, "Just keep walking. It's enough of us in a group to make sure we are okay." The driver side car window started rolling down. A guy put his head out the window. He said, "Excuse me, will you come talk to me for a second?" We looked at each other from girl to girl. Not knowing whom he was speaking to. He parked his car, and we all continued walking. This guy opened his car door and got out of the car.

Q Was His Name

He walked to the left side of the group of girls. He grabbed my hand. I snatched it back. He said, "Hi. I didn't mean any harm. I just want to get to know you. My name is Q." I was still reluctant to tell him my name. I wasn't having relationships outside of us girls. We taught each other to always be cautious. Then he said, "Do you have a name?" I said yes but still not telling him. He continued to walk with us engaging in conversations with the girls and me. He left his car half a block down the street to walk with us. We made it to the candy lady's house. I knocked on the door of the candy house. The owner came to take our orders. Once everyone ordered their sodas, pickles, candies, and chips, Q ordered a soda. He told all the girls, "I got it."

He Got the Bankroll

Q pulled out a big wad of money and paid the candy lady for all the items that we purchased. The four other girls that we were walking with, my sisters, and I started whispering in my ear. They were telling me who he was. They lived in that very neighborhood from when they were small. We were new to the area. One of the girls said, "Girl, you better talk to him. He got that money." I blew it off. That wasn't of my caliber. We grew up without money our entire lives. Money was not one of the things we wished for as kids. Once he paid for everyone's goodies, it's like they were sold. They started walking ahead of Q and me. They were letting him have alone time with me. He asked, "So are you gone tell me your name?" I said, "My name is TyshAnn." He said, "Okay. Now I have something to go on." He took a genuine interest in me. He wanted to know all my likes, dislikes, what made me laugh, smile, and cry. He wanted to know my pet peeves and everything. At this time, there never was a self-evaluation done of myself. I never thought about the things that I liked or didn't. We didn't grow up with many choices. All those questions he asked me, I'd never thought about until then.

Steak and lobster

He asked me if I wanted to take a ride with him. I said, "Only if my sisters can go too." He said, "Cool." When we made it back to his car, my sisters were the waiting like guard dogs. I don't know where the other girls disappeared to. Elijah had her own thing going on, so she told to Kymara to ride with us. Q walked around to the passenger side door. He opened the door for me and allowed me to sit in the seat. He shut the door behind me. Kymara opened the back passenger door. She got in, and he made it to the driver side and got in the car. The first place he took us was to a steak and lobster restaurant. When we got back to the car, he asked us what type of music we liked. Neither of us said anything. He put a cassette tape in the deck. When the music turned on, the bass went boom. We drove around town. Every place or house he went to, we didn't stay long. He knew everyone all over the town. Q started introducing me to everyone that we met as his li'l mama. I didn't know what that was. It was the first time I heard it. I just stayed quiet and went along with the ride. He drove us home. Q parked in the parking lot that was adjacent to our house. Kymara got out of the car and went into the house. Q told me he enjoyed being around me and wanted to hang out again. He gave me his home number and told me to call him.

Illegal Endeavors

Over the next ten months, Q and I hung out. He was very generous with money and gifts. Every time he would see me, he'd come bearing gifts. I enjoyed the times I would have when I was with him. I became accustomed to living life with him. I wondered what he did for a living, but I didn't ask. I assumed it had to be something illegal because he never talked about working a job or punching a clock. One day, we stopped by one of the houses that he frequented. He told me he would be right back. He got out of the car. I saw a dark shadow run across the yard of the house we were parked in front of. I just knew someone was trying to pull a jack move.

Robberies in the Area

Robberies were occurring a lot in the area. Before I could look left and alert him to what I'd just seen, I heard a helicopter hovering. I saw a black suburban with black tinted windows. It was presidential style. Then I saw a black Crown Victoria with black tint. It had police lights on it. The lights were on and flashing. Both vehicles swooped in to block us in. Four men wearing all black jumped out of the suburban. They had guns. They were all screaming, "PUT YOUR HANDS ABOVE YOUR HEAD!" Q put his hands above his head. The men rushed in to subdue him. They made him put his hands behind his back and placed handcuffs on him. Two of the men walked Q to the crown Victoria. They placed him in the car and shut the door. The other two men walked around to the passenger seat where I was sitting. They informed me that they were the feds.

They Got Who They Came For

One of the gentlemen expressed to me that they had been watching Q for the past three years. They told me I had nothing to worry about. They told me that they got who they came for. I was in disbelief. I didn't expect the day to turn bad like it did. I watched the feds drive off with him in the back seat of the car.

Get the Feds Out of My Sight

I made sure the feds were out of sight. I walked around to the driver seat of the car. I got in the car and adjusted the seat. The keys were still in the ignition. I turned the key. I proceeded and drove home. I proceeded to drive home. When I got home, the phone rang. When I picked up, I heard an automated woman's voice saying, "You have a free call from an inmate at the federal corrections facility. To accept this call, press one. To decline this call—" Before I could hear the rest of the automated call, I quickly pressed the number one button to accept the call. The automated woman said, "Your free call will begin. You have fifteen minutes remaining." On the other end of the phone, I heard Q say, "Hey Ty. I'm sorry that you had to experience that. I never told you what was going on before. I thought the less you knew the better it would be for both of us. Thank you for being such a beautiful person to me. I have a feeling I'm going to be in here for a long time. I had so many plans for you and me, but I ran out of time. I need to ask you to do something for me." I said, "What is that?" He started talking in code. I wondered why, but the longer I paid attention, I understood. He asked me to drive his car to Alexander Street in two days at 6: 30 p.m. He told me to park in the apartments behind the church. He told me his aunt would meet me over there. I said, "Okay." For the next two days, I went to school like it was a normal day. The only difference was I was driving his car.

Follow Instruction

On that second day, I followed the instructions he'd given. I didn't know what I was getting into. I just knew that I felt deeply for him, and if there was a chance that I could help him in his situation, I would. When I parked in the apartments behind the church, a car pulled up beside me. Q's aunt was in the car with another guy. His aunt got in the car with me. She showed me a funny shaped key on the set of keys that were on Q's key ring. She told me that Q asked her to ask me if I remembered where the salvage yard was. She said, "He went to it when he needed parts for his car." I said yes. She said, "Well, Q needs you to go to the salvage yard and find a broken-down Cadillac. The Cadillac will be the same year as this Cadillac you are driving." Then she said, "The only difference would be that the Cadillac in the junk yard is green." She got out of the car with me and into the car she was in and drove away. I drove to the salvage yard. I remembered where it was because I paid attention to everything when I was with him. I never got out of the car when we frequented these places unless he asked me to. I got out of the car and walked toward the office building. I began speaking to the front office attendant.

An older man with silver hair on his head and face came from the back office to the front attendant desk. He said, "I already know who you are. Come on back." Then he said, "I'm Pawpaw Franko." He informed me that he was Q's grandpa, and he was the owner of the salvage yard. I walked with him to the back office. The back office had a back door that lead to the outside and back of the building. When we walked out of the back door, we walked into the salvage yard. The salvage yard was so big. It extended for two acres or so. There were hundreds of savaged cars. He instructed me to follow him. I followed him. As I followed him, he talked. He said, "He was modest when he told me about how beautiful you were. You are gorgeous." I said, "Thank you." He went on to say, "I know that you are special, and he trusts you 'cause if he didn't, we wouldn't be here." I didn't know what else to say. It seemed as if everyone knew of me, but I didn't know much of anything. He continued to talk and shoot flirting comments. I was almost offended. After walking half a mile, we stopped at a yellow Cadillac. This was the one his aunt described. Pawpaw Franko said, "I will leave you to this." Before walking away, he said, "Now remember, I'm his grandpa. If he ain't man enough, I will gladly be your man." In my mind, I thought, *Oh my God*. Pawpaw Franko walked away leaving me with the car.

The Gym Bag

I looked all round and inside of the car. The car was clean. What was it that he wanted me to get from the car? He didn't leave much instruction. There were five keys on the set of keys he gave me with a flashlight on a key ring. None of them fit any doors on this car. I was becoming frustrated. I walked to the trunk of the car. I tried every key into the key hole on the trunk. I placed the finale key on the set of keys into the key hole on the trunk. The finale key was the funny shaped key that Q's aunt pointed out to me earlier that day. Finally, the key turned, and the trunk popped up. I was relieved to have found the correct key. I didn't know what to expect. I looked in the trunk of the car. It was clean. I lifted the vinyl where the spare tire and jack would be. There was no spare tire. There was a burnt orange long horns duffle bag. The bag was dirty. It looked worn. There were a pair of black Chuck Taylors next to the bag. I unzipped the bag. Inside the bag, I found a toothbrush, toothpaste, a small face towel, and men's anti-perspirant spray.

Illegal Substance

I continued going through the bag. I found change of clothes and a big dry off towel. Underneath the towel was a Jordan shoebox. Inside the shoebox was stacks of ten one hundred dollar bills. The stacks of money were wrapped in rubber bands. All this money, I thought, *What does he want me to do with it?* Next to the shoebox was a little gun. It was a twenty-two. It was custom-made. It had little red and purple roses all over it. I picked it up to check and see if it was loaded. It was loaded with ten bullets. Safety was off. I put the safety on and then put the gun back into the bag. I continued to look in the bag. I found two separate ziplock bags. Each ziplock bag contained four hard white circular things that resembled a sugar cookie. I did not know what this was. What was I to do with this stuff? I decided to leave the cookie things in the bag. They were too hard to be sugar cookies. I wasn't ready to deal with whatever those things were. I hid the ziplock under the vinyl in the corner of the truck on the Cadillac. I pulled the duffle bag out of the trunk I was a little paranoid about the money. I decided to put the gun in my pants pocket. It was small enough to fit. I carried the duffle bag out of the salvage yard.

Li'l Duffle Bag Girl

I placed the duffle bag inside of the trunk under my spare tire. I made sure I went straight home. No stops along the way. When I got home, I heard the phone ring. I picked up the phone. It was Pawpaw Franko. He had Q on a three-way call. I guess that was a confirmation call. Pawpaw Franko said, "Hold on, gorgeous. He wants to talk to you." I heard him say, "I see you met my grandpa." I said yes. Pawpaw Franko said, "Yeah, I met her! We got plans of running away and getting married." The two of them laughed at the same time. I couldn't find the humor. Q changed the subject. He said, "Did you get everything?" I said, "Yes, everything except for the ziplock." He said, "No! You need everything. I need you to get that!" Pawpaw Franko said, "Don't worry about it. I can pick up the keys from her tomorrow while she is at school. I will take it to her when she gets home." He said, "Okay. That will be cool." Then he said, "I really appreciate you. Once you have everything, stay in contact with my grandpa." I said, "Okay."

OG Status

As scheduled, Pawpaw Franko came to the school on my lunch break and retrieved the funny shaped key. When I made it home, Pawpaw Franko was waiting in the driveway. I pulled up in the driveway, parked my car, and got into his car. He brought the contents of the ziplock bags to me. When I thought about the money, I thought he wanted me to use the money to pay for him a lawyer or something so he could get out of jail. That was only half of it. Q wanted me to take five thousand of the ten thousand dollars to pay a lawyer and put three thousand on his books. He wanted me to keep two thousand for myself. I thought to myself, *Okay. That will work*. Then Pawpaw went on to explain the contents in the ziplock.

Sugar Cookies

They were not cookies. Each was a whole ounce of rock cocaine. I could not believe that was what those sugar cookies were. It was the first-time I'd ever seen it in that form. I've seen it in the powder form. I've even seen it in rock form. I didn't know that the little ten dollar and twenty dollar piece of rock came from a whole cookie rock. Hell, I never wondered about the theory on rock cocaine. He had a glass plate and a pow razor blade on the plate. He took one of the cookies out the bag. He proceeded to show me how to cut the entire ounce down.

Cookie Cutter

Pawpaw Franko cut the cookie into two equal halves. He told me I would sell those as halves. Then he cut one of the halves into quarters. He told me I would sell those as quarters. He showed me how to cut the quarter down to the ten and twenty dollar crack pieces that I was familiar with. He finally reached the part of what I was supposed to do with the cookies. I was completely disappointed. I was hurt. I didn't allow Pawpaw Franko to see my emotion. I just went with the flow. Q wanted me to continue building on what he had started. He wanted me to continue servicing his clientele. His reason was to keep him and me with money. I thought, *Who the hell does he think he is?* He got me fucked up. How could he care for me if he would put me in such a dangerous situation? I was in raged. Over the next few days, I followed instruction to all his request. I paid the lawyer and put the money on his books. I thought to myself, *Well maybe I can get rid of this stuff. Once I am done I won't get any more.*

Money and Power

I didn't know the value of money. I grew up poor. Q invited me into a whole new luxurious world. I became accustomed to having the things that came with money. I cut ninety-nine crack rocks out of one of the cookies. I made fourteen hundred dollars out of one cookie, rock for rock. I sent Q four thousand dollars. I know that wasn't the way he intended it. I gained my own intentions. I estimated the value of the eight zones and sent him the street value amount. In my mind, I was paying him off. A year passed. I was a miniature queenpin in my community. By this time, I was getting ready to graduate high school. I went to school to finish what I started. I wanted to prove to others and myself that I would graduate. As soon as the school bell rung, I was in grind mode. I wasn't like the average high schoolers planning for college. I already had a degree. It was getting money in the streets. I didn't trust anyone. The only people I allowed to ride in my car were my sisters. We were popular because we had the best of everything. Every time the latest shoes came out, my sisters and I got them. The latest clothes, other fashions, etc., we got them. I was a week from graduation. I was making more money than the principal. I was only seventeen. Everything was going well. I paid crack smokers to do everything that I didn't feel like doing. I felt like street royalty.

Delta 88

I decided that it was time for me to get my own place. I had just turned seventeen. I wasn't quite old enough to put my name on a lease. I paid one of my smokers with good credit to lease a house for me. She wasn't a dope fiend. She was a smoker. There was a difference. I trusted her more than I trusted anyone. On graduation day, I was moving into my new place. The clientele that Q left me were consistent. I felt like I was living the high life. I pulled up at the gas station to put gas in my car. I went into the convenience store to pay for gas. I came out of the store. I went to my car and began pumping my gas. I noticed a black Delta 88 with tinted window in the parking lot. I saw through the front window that two men were sitting in the car with the headlights off. I didn't pay it too much attention. I was excited about being able to move into my new place. Once I pumped the gas, I got in my car, cut up the music, and drove off. I noticed that the Delta 88 pulled out of the parking lot as soon as I did.

Hater Got Me Wrong

A few blocks up were a shopping center, I pulled in to see if the car would continue following me. It did. I stopped my car. The car pulled beside me. The passenger window came down. It was someone I knew. A buster ass nigga that was always bumbing and roaching. He hustled also but he had a sherm habit. He had money sometimes, but his habit for PCP and marijuana got the best of him. I rolled my window down all the way. He asked me where I was headed. I said, "Riding. Why? What's up?" He said nothing and proceeded to get out the car. I didn't trust anyone. What did this nigga want? He asked me if I talked to Q. I wondered why he was asking me about Q. They didn't deal with each other when Q was out of jail. I was a young woman having more money than half these niggas out in the streets. I knew somebody would be in their feelings. That's why I didn't hang around anyone. If someone was riding with me, it would be my smoker (LoLo) because she is going to stuff the work when Five-O came. The smokers kept my money coming. If I kept them close, when I gave them dope to sell, they were going to make sure I got my money. When he proceeded walking to the car, I thought to drive off, but I didn't want them to follow me. I chose to stay there and hear the nigga out. He leaned on my car door. He said, "What's up, Ty? Why you are looking all crazy?" I said, "My nigga, what's up? What do you want?" He pulled on my shirt and said, "GET UP OUT THIS CAR!" I saw that he didn't have a weapon or anything. He thought just because I was a petite framed female and there was no Q around to protect me, I would be an easy target. I said, "You want me to get out the car?" He said, "YEAH. GET UP OUT THE CAR!" I said, "Okay. Let me go." He released my shirt. I quickly reached down under my seat where my 22 was sitting. Before I could aim the gun in the right direction, he was running. The person in the car he was with was speeding away. The driver of the car almost left him. I fired four shots. I was aiming for his head. He was ducking and jumping over cars, trying to catch up with the car that was leaving him. He finally caught up to the car. He was in. The passenger door flew opened for him, and they burned off.

My New Job

I was a little rattled by what had just transpired. I drove cautiously to my new place. Settling into my new place was good for my glow up. A week into my new place, I started thinking on a more grown up level. I knew when things were good, and when you were doing wrong, anything could turn for worst. I thought to myself, *What was I going to do with myself besides hustle?* I needed a cover-up. I began a job at a barbecue restaurant. I worked there for a year. I worked at the restaurant from nine to five. As soon as work was over, I went home to bathe and change clothes. I was back in grind mode, selling dope. One day while I was working at the restaurant, this group of four guys came in the restaurant. They ordered barbecue to go. I took their orders and provided their food. Two of the guys were trying to figure if I had a boyfriend. I took an interest in the milder mannered one. The other guy was too flashy. He kept pulling out wads of money, trying to outdo the other guys. That turned me off. I think the wads of money gave me flash backs of Q. I didn't have much conversation with the flashy one. I gave my pager number to the one with that was milder mannered. I got to know him. I invited him to my place. By this time, I was tired of the risk that came with selling drugs. I was always looking over my shoulders. I didn't have any personal relationships outside of my sisters because I didn't know who to trust. I was ready to try another route. My spirit started speaking to me. I began to get convicted about selling drugs to my people. I thought to myself, *I don't think I want to do this any longer.*

JT and Me

JT was my new guy's name. After hanging out and spending a lot of time together, JT asked me how I felt about him. I told him I cared for him a lot. He asked me if I would be his woman. I said yes. I informed him about my lifestyle. I confided in him all my secrets. I didn't want him to find out any other way. I showed him my stash with all the drugs and money. I told him once everything was sold, I was done with that way of living. He volunteered to help me get rid of it. He said this way we could get rid of it faster. I sold everything I had. I sold it in five months. I accomplished my goal. I was no longer a drug dealer. I could live my life to its fullest potential. JT and I were getting along well. For some reason, I didn't feel like myself. My thoughts were always scattered. I had a hard time focusing. My patience was thin. What was wrong with me? I scheduled an appointment with my doctor. The doctor told me that my iron was low. I felt relieved that was all that was wrong with me, but then he walked back into the room with a different information sheet. He revealed to me that I was ten weeks pregnant. I knew what would happen when a man and women is together without protection, but I didn't think I would get pregnant or even if I could. I never thought about it to be honest. I called JT from the doctor's office. He came right away. He was excited about what was to come. He was very supportive. I started putting all my focus toward bringing a healthy baby into the world. JT gave me all the money that he made off the work I gave him. I assumed that meant he was sold out.

He's Changing

Although things were going well in my life, I often felt like I had scatterbrain. My thoughts and emotions were always so scattered at that moment. I didn't notice, JT was changing. He was making more purchases and staying out late. He purchased chirp phones for us. They were like walkie-talkies. It was 8:00 a.m. I was eight months into my pregnancy. JT and I were in the bed sleeping. I was awakened from a woman's voice. She chirped through over the chirp phone. She was so loud. I woke up out of my sleep in a panic because I thought my past was catching up to me. I thought some cops were on a bull horn outside of our house or something. I jumped up quickly to see what the hell was going on. I cut the volume down on the chirp phone. I could clearly hear the woman saying, "You better tell her or I will." I woke him up out of his sleep to address the situation.

Who Is This Bitch?

I asked him, "What is going on? Who is this BITCH?" He had the nerve to tell me it was someone he was selling work to. That was when I found out he was still selling drugs. I had him call the number back and address what it was she was speaking of telling me. JT put the phone on speaker. He was so nervous. He couldn't even get the words out of his mouth once the woman started talking. She went on to say that when JT and I got into an argument three months ago… JT cursed her out. He said, "Bitch, I told you that I had a wife, and that we were just on bad terms." He went on telling her that he used her for that night, and that she didn't mean shit to him. I was shocked to hear him speak like that to a woman. I was happy that he put her in her place, but I never saw him to be that type of guy. Boy was I wrong. JT hung up in her face. When he hung up the phone with her, he said, "Ty, I have something to tell you. I'm scared I'm going to lose you." I was nervously anticipating what he had to say. I had so many butter-flies in my stomach. I thought I was going to shit on myself.

Angry Me

All the mixed emotions angered me. I was ready to go to war. He told me that he had an intimate night with not only that women but two other women. He told me that he'd been doing party drugs like ecstasy and smoking sherm sticks while partying with his homeboys and these women. He told me that he got caught up in the fast lane. He said, "Fast money brings fast hoes and parties." As soon as he said that, I slapped him in the mouth. Before I could slap him again, he grabbed my hands and pinned me down on the bed. I was so hurt and angry. I was kicking and screaming, trying to get him to release me. He laid on the top part of my body being careful not to smash my belly. Why did he wait to act like this once I got pregnant? I hated him for a few days. I put him out of the house. He did everything he could to get back in my good grace. On the tenth day, he brought a bunch of items for the baby. By this time, I was calmed enough to have a civil conversation with him. We decided to work it out. He said he didn't want his baby to grow up without him. He told me that he would never cheat, do party drugs, or sell any more drugs. I took his word for it.

Jacob Arrives

We had our first son. Together we named him Jacob. JT had one son prior to us meeting. We had a good family setting. I didn't see any signs of the drug use, drug dealing, or party women. He went to worked and came straight home most of the time. Everything was going smooth. Two years had passed, I was pregnant with our second son. Everything was consistent. We were happy. One Friday after work, I picked up my son from day care. We went home. I put him to bed early because I was tired. I went to sleep at approximately 8:10 p.m. My phone began ringing off the hook at 1:30 a.m. I got three missed calls. I called the number back at 1:35 a.m. I heard a bunch of screaming in the background. I said, "Hello who is this? What is going on?" It was JT's brother's wife. She told me to hurry over to her house. It was an emergency with JT.

PCP + Embalming = Sherm Head

When I got Jacob and myself situated in the car, we dove to my sister-in-law's house. When I pulled up to her house, JT was running down the street naked. He stopped in someone's yard. He ran to their water hose and started letting the water hose run on his head. He started screaming, "I'M ON FIRE! I'M ON FIRE!" It was unlike anything I'd ever seen before. I was so angry at him. But I felt bad at the same time. I almost felt as if everything was my fault. His friends that were riding in the car with him were laughing. I asked JT's brother's wife to give me a blanket. Then I asked her to watch Jacob for me. He was strapped in the car seat sleeping. I walked down the street with the blanket and towel. When I got to the yard, I began calling his name. It was like he got an instant reality check when he saw my face. He dropped the water hose. I turned it off. I told him to dry off with the towel. I covered him with the blanket. I got him get in the car with me and took him home.

Jerome Arrives

These types of mishaps continued to happen. I gave birth to our second son Jerome. The fighting between us increased and became severe. I needed to leave this situation. I had a small kid and a baby. JT was still selling drugs and doing them. One Sunday morning, I got up early and went to church. Everything that the pastor preached about seemed to pertain to me and my situation. I cried the entire church service. I knew that it was time for a change. I had to get away from JT. I asked him to leave our home. He refused. When the kids and I arrived home from church that Sunday, I walked into our house. I saw that every piece of furniture was flipped over or broken. It looked like a tornado flew around my living room. I walked the boys to their room. I saw that their room was in perfect order. I put Jerome in his crib. He was still sleeping. Then I put Jacob in his play pen. It was time for his nap also. Once I got the babies settled, I walked out of the boy's room and shut the door behind me.

False Imprisonment

I continued to investigate the rest of the house. My bedroom was just as bad as the living room. All my clothes were cut up or thrown out the back window. I had a feeling who done it, but I wasn't sure until I saw my clothes cut up and scattered. I instantly knew it was JT. He did stupid things like that when he was high or hurting. I was sick and tired of him and his actions. I went to the retrieve the house phone from the wall in the kitchen. I took the cordless phone off the wall. I walked over to the front window that outlooked the front yard. I listened for the dial tone. I was going to call the cops. I wanted him away from me. I knew the only way that would happen without anyone getting hurt was for him to go to jail. I pressed 9 on the phone. Before I could press 1 1, the phone hung up. JT snatched the phone out of my hands. I was scared and surprised. I didn't know where he came from. All the doors in the house were locked. I didn't hear anyone come in.

I Can't Breathe

He caught me off guard. He asked me, "Who are you calling?" I told him I was calling my mom. I had to think quick. I didn't want him to know I was calling the cops on him. I could tell he was on drugs. He talked clear when he wasn't under the influence. When he was under the influence, his words dragged. I reached to get the phone out of his hand. He put his arm up over my head as if he was playing keep away with me. I became angered. I turned to walk away. JT grabbed me from behind and put me in a choke hold. I saw a lamp on the floor, but it was too low to grab. I wanted him to think he was putting me in a sleep. I allowed my legs to bend under me as if I was passing out. He continued holding me, but he went down to the floor with me. When I got to the floor, I felt as if I was about to faint. I thought to myself, *He is about to sleep me. I can't make it.* I felt my oxygen cutting off. I closed my eyes to see the black behind my eyelids. I felt his breath on the back of my ear. He whispered, "I am going to KILL you!"

Popped in the Head

I reached to my right where I remembered the lamp to be. I picked up the lamp and pulled it behind my head where he was behind me. I popped him in the head so hard with the lamp that it shattered into a bunch of pieces. He instantly freed me. I ran for the phone. He ran away with blood pouring out of his head. I called 9-1-1. Two squad cars came. The officers took statements and pictures, but they made no arrest. JT had time to get far away from the area. A group called Victim Services came out. They gave me information about a safe place. The safe place was a shelter that was used to hide victims of domestic crimes. The kids and I went to live in the domestic violence victim shelter.

Accomplished

The shelter helped me a lot. They funded all the goals I wanted to accomplish. I wanted to become a hairstylist. The shelter funded it, so I went to cosmetology school and obtained my cosmetology license. I saw myself accomplishing everything I set out to accomplish. I had no distractions, drama, or drugs in my life. The accomplishment came easily. We lived in the shelter for six months. During our stay in the shelter, JT's mom called my cell phone. She started the conversation asking how we were doing. I told her everything was going well. I thought her son put her up to calling me to see if he could find out where we were, but instead she told me that he had been arrested and sentenced. He was arrested on drug charges. The judge sentenced him to twenty-two months in prison. I was relieved in a way. I hoped the time-out in jail would bring him back to the JT he used to be before he got caught up in the drug world. I prayed and hoped he would come out a different person and better father to his children.

A Safe Place

Now I could leave the shelter. I had to find a new place for me and the children to live in. The shelter assisted me in moving my things out of the old place and storage placement. My lease at my old place was up. The shelter continued paying my rent on the old place until the lease was up. They didn't want me to get any broken lease because of the domestic situation. After a month of searching for a new place to call home and begin a new start, I found the perfect place. I found a three-bedroom with plenty of backyard space for my sons to play. The rooms were huge with plenty of space. The shelter funded moving truck services and movers.

Moving Day

This day was the big day. The owner finalized the lease. We were given the okay to move into our new place. The helpers from the shelter and the movers did all the work. They did not want me to lift a finger. I felt like God's favour. It reminded me of old days when I felt like royalty. The big difference now was that I was not doing anything illegal. I didn't have to look over my shoulders. I was all the way legit. I was happy and content. We were moving into our new home. I got the key from the landlord. Once I did a walk-through of the house, I made a list of all the things we would need starting off new.

Household Needs

I drove to the Dollar store to purchase all my household needs from cleaning supplies, toiletries, and hygiene things. Upon walking in the store, I tried to reach for a basket with my right hand. The task was a little complex. I had my two-and-a-half-year-old son, Jacob's hand with my left hand. I was holding my eleven-month-old son, Jerome on my right hip. I couldn't get a full grip on the basket. I extended my foot to the bottom of the basket, then I pulled it close enough to me. I let go of Jacob's hand to put Jerome in the basket. After I put Jerome in the basket, I bent down to pick Jacob up to put him in the back of the basket. As soon as I bent down to lift Jacob, this guy rushed to my side. He asked me, "Do you need any help?" I said, "Oh no, thank you! I got it." I continued strolling through the store picking up our items. When I finished shopping, I paid for our items. Then the kids and I made our way back to the car. I unlocked the car doors. I put Jacob in the back seat and made sure his safety belt was securely strapped around him.

Stranger

When I looked up to grab Jerome, the same guy from inside the store was standing there asking me if he could help me. He was beginning to freak me out. I pictured the scene from the scary movies where you get five feet away from the killer to look up and find that he just popped up in front of you. I told him, "You scared the crap out of me." He said, "I didn't get your name." I said, "I didn't give it." I guess he saw that I was on the defense. Then he said he admired my strength and how phenomenal I was with. I didn't know what he was talking about or referring to. He said, "The way that you care for you children while still taking care of your business." I wasn't flattered at all. I felt like I was doing just what I was supposed to be doing. I didn't see a need for all the extra recognition.

No Trust

I was used to not trusting anyone. I thought everyone was always up to something. He asked me if there was a church that I attended. I said, "Yes, different ones on occasion." He said, "Oh okay. I attend Tabernacle Church." He went on to say that the church had a toddler and infant ministry for children my kids ages. He said, "You should come visit one day." He gave me his card. I said, "Okay, thank you." I continued doing what I was doing. I was hoping that he would take the cue and leave me alone. I put my son, Jerome, in his car seat. The stranger walked off. Once I got Jerome strapped in his car seat, I proceeded to put our buys into the trunk of the car until the shopping cart was empty. I was looking for somewhere close by to ditch my shopping cart. I didn't want to go too far away from my car. As I was looking around, the stranger walked back up. He was pushing his basket. It was empty. He reached over and grab my basket also. He said, "I will take it for you." I said, "Thank you. I am appreciative." I got in my car and drove off. I made it to my house in the nick of time the movers were just arriving. They needed me to be home to let them in. I unlocked the doors, and they got all our things moved in. The boys and I slept comfortably in our new place in our own beds. That was a good night.

My Life

Over the next few months, we were getting stable. I was making our house into a comfortable home for the boys and me. My cosmetology license was valid. I applied for a stylist/barber position around the corner from my new house, and I got the position. I decided to put the boys in a day care across the street from where I got hired as a barber/stylist. I started making good, decent money. I did all of this without drugs or drug money. I was humbled and no longer accustomed to getting all the things I wanted. I lived off the things that we really needed. Every now and then, I might treat myself. I was happy, surviving, and thriving. I was getting back to me. My peace of mind was better than it had ever been before. More time passed. Before I knew it, I'd been working on the same job for two and a half years. I earned my seniority on the job. I was considered a master stylist. In November, our store had undergone a remodel.

Grand Opening

All the store owners and managers got together. They thought that we should have a grand opening. The owner decided to have a grand opening the week before Christmas. Our store had discounts and mark-downs on everything. This was one of the busiest times for the entire shopping center. I did tons of clients that week. Friday was the last day of the grand opening sales and specials. I cut hair for twenty-one people on that day. I was tired and ready to go home. On Fridays, we closed at five clock in the afternoon. It was five minutes until five. Everyone was cleaning up and getting ready to close their stations. I heard the bell ring on the entrance door. The bell went off when some-one walked in or out. When the bell rung, all the stylist looked at the door to see who was entering.

Last Minute Frustration

We were all hoping it was not a client needing a haircut. The client walked in and asked, "What time do you all close? Do you have time for one more haircut?" I was cursing him out in my mind. Because we went by a system that went in order, and it was now my turn. I pulled all my tools for cleaning and cutting back out. When the customer came back to sit in my chair, he looked familiar. But I didn't recognize him. He had so much hair on his face and his head. I cut his hair nice and clean. Then I could see his face clearly.

The Stranger

It was the stranger from the Dollar store a couple years ago. I thought to myself, *Just my luck.* He wasn't as talkative or persistent as he was when I saw him at the Dollar store. His spirits were low. I sparked up a conversation for good customer service. I asked him how he was enjoying the holidays. He said, "I'm not." Then he went to a long story of one unfortunate event after another. The first event that he told me was his mom was dying. Then he said his brother had just passed two days ago. I told him to stand fast and keep faith in God's word. He looked at me with tears swelling in his eyes. He said, "I'm trying." Then he went on to tell me that he worked in the electrical field. I think he just needed a listening ear to hear, so I listened to him talk until my job was done. He thanked me for cutting his hair so late. He told me he felt much better. It was protocol to give the customers our individual business cards because we were independent contractors. I gave him my card and took him to the cash register for the receptionist to cash out his service ticket. I told him to have a nice weekend, and that I would be praying for everything to get better for him. Then I walked back to my station to clean up the hair. His hair cut was twenty-four dollars. The receptionist brought a tip to me of seventy-six dollars. I had to make sure she hadn't made a mistake. I thanked him again as he went out the door. Then I put the seventy-six dollars in my smock pocket with the rest of the tips I'd earned for that day. I went home feeling successful.

Unexpected Phone Call

I picked up my boys from day care. Once we made it home, I fed them, gave them baths, and put them in the bed. I was just about to unwind myself. My cell phone rang. I didn't notice the number. I didn't give my number to anyone unless it was for business. I wondered who could be calling at this time. My business hours were between the hours of nine and five. I answered the call. I heard a voice say, "Hello, Ty." I hadn't heard this voice in a long time, but it was familiar. It was JT, my children's father. The last time I spoke to him was when he had me in a choke hold. I didn't know how to feel. He asked me how I'd been doing. He told me that he got sentenced to twenty-two months, but they also made him do a drug treatment program. I asked him how he got my number. That was baffling to me because I went off the radar. After I came out of the shelter, I didn't keep in contact with his family or mines.

Word of Advertisement

He told me that he went to get his haircut at the barber shop that he'd been going to since he was a kid. Then he said his regular barber was not there, so he let a substitute cut his hair. The substitute messed his hair up. Someone who was in the barber shop marketing his business had one of my cards. The card holder referred me. I thought to myself, *Damn. Now he knows where I work. I hope he is not on that bullshit.* He told me that he wanted to see his children. I told him to have his mom contact me, and we could arrange a visit. I told him and his mom that I would meet him if she was with him. We would have to meet in a busy space like the park or something. He agreed to the terms.

Meeting Spot

I met with him and his mom once a week at the park. He asked me if he could take them with him one day. I said, "I must see how everything plays out. If you continue to stay clean and do the right thing, we will arrange it." We continued this way for six months. The seventh month he told me he had a job. I was proud of him. He was really turning a new leaf. I asked him if he had been staying clean away from drugs. He said, "Yes, my job does random drug test." I was like, "Okay. That sounds good." The eight month, he asked me if they could spend the weekend with him. I wasn't quite sure if I was ready for that. I told him to keep doing good, and I would come around.

All Is Well

A year passed. It was Christmas time again. Jacob was almost seven years old. He articulated very well. He was really smart, very spiritual, and analytical. He knew right from wrong. He could relay and repeat everything exactly the way it happened. Besides he was very overprotective of his little brother. I agreed to allow JT to keep his children. He told me to bring them to his mom's house after I picked them up from day care. I took them home and gathered their overnight bags. I took them to JT's mom's house. JT's sister was there with her two children. I felt a lot more secure. I asked where his mom was. He said she would be gone to visit family for the weekend. I handed to him their overnight bags. Then I kissed Jacob and Jerome goodbye. I walked out of the door.

Flirtatious Comments

When I got to my car, my phone began to ring. I answered it. JT was on the other line. He said, "Baby mama, you sure is fine?" I laughed. Then I said, "Dude, get off my line. Take care of my babies." He said, "Of course, they are my babies too." He continued with flirting comments. My other line started beeping. I cut JT's flirtatious conversation short. I said, "Hey, I must talk to you later. My other line is beeping." I hung up with JT to answer the other line. The voice sounded familiar, but I didn't know who it was. The voice said, "Hey, miss lady, how are you?" I said, "Who is this?" He said, "Senoj." I said, "Sen na who?" He said, "I came to the barber shop five minutes until five." I still didn't remember, then he said, "I left the seventy-six-dollar tip." I remembered then, but I continued to act like I didn't know. He said, "You don't remember? I met you at the Dollar store a couple of years before that I gave you my card." I said, "Oh okay. I know who you are." He said, "I'm good, how are you?" I said, "I can't complain. What can I do for you?" He said, "Can I schedule an appointment with you for next Friday?" I said, "Sure, as long as you don't come in five minutes until close." We both laughed.

Call Your Bluff

Then he said, "Do you think I could see you outside of work? I would like to take you on a date." I got quiet because I wasn't expecting him to ask me that. I appreciated the straight forwardness. I thought about what he said he did for a living. He wasn't a drug dealer. From what I remembered, he was a man of God. I was thinking. He said, "Did I scare you away?" I said, "No. I was just thinking." He said, "So what do you think?" I said, "Sure, how about now?" Senoj got choked up. With hesitation and stammer in his words, he said, "Right... right now?" I said, "Yes. Now, where would you like to meet?" He said, "I would need to go home to change." I said, "No you don't. We can walk through the park and talk. No need to dress up or change." He kept on insisting that he needed to go home. To me that said enough about him. I was very analytical. I said, "Okay. You go home, and I will catch you later." He said, "Okay." I thought to myself, *I will be busy later*. I went home cuddled under my blanket and read a good book until I went to sleep. I spent my weekend catching up on sleep.

Pick up Time

It was Sunday. I called JT. I told him that I would be over at 8:00 p.m. to pick up the boys. He said, "Okay. They will be ready." Eight o'clock rolled around. I was running a little behind. I decided to pick up a few items from the grocery store before I picked my sons up. I made it to JT's mom's house at 8:35 p.m. I got out of my car and locked the doors. I'd missed my boys. I was happy it was time to pick them up. I was relieved that their dad was finally getting his stuff together. I needed him to be a good father to his children. I walked up the driveway. I think they heard me coming 'cause before I could knock on the front door, JT opened the front door. The kids ran up to me and hugged me as if they were missing me just as much as I was missing them. After I got all the hugs and kisses from my boys, JT motioned for me to follow him into the den That's where he had the boys overnight bags.

Knock at the Door

I went to retrieve my boy's things. The doorbell rang. JT went to answer the door. I heard a loud thud. It sounded like someone dropped something on a hardwood floor in an empty house. I walked toward the front door to see what the noise was. When I walked into the living room, I saw JT lying on the floor on his stomach. He was begging. "Please, man, don't kill me. Please, don't kill me." A dark skinned black man that looked to be six feet tall, one three hundred and something pounds was standing over JT with a gun. When the man realized I had walked into the living room, he became startled. He quickly rose the gun to my face. When he looked into my eyes, I saw a look of remorse. I read his lips. They said DAMN! He took gun out of my face. He aimed the gun down back on JT.

Victimized

I was maybe five to six steps to the left of JT and the assailant. When I looked to the right of JT, my son Jacob was six or seven steps to his right. My heart shook. I forgot he'd followed his dad into the living area. When my eyes settled at Jacob's face, Jacob was crying and praying. I couldn't hear anything that was coming out of his mouth, but I could read his lips. He had both hands in front of him compressed together. He was saying, "God, please help us." Then he looked at me with his hands in a prayer saying, "Mama, please help us." That moment appeared to be going in slow motion as if it had been chopped and screwed.

Survival Instincts

When I looked at his face, my instinct to survive kicked in. I ran into the kitchen. The sink was full of dirty dishes. I was looking for a knife. I couldn't find one. It seemed like everything was moving so fast. I didn't have any time to have an emotion. My thinking and movement were quick. It's as if I turned into a robot. I couldn't hear anything. Everything I could see was in a shade of red. I opened the dishwasher. I saw a small steak knife. Without thought, I rushed back into the living room area. The only thing I saw was an oversized black-white shadow with a red target on it. By this time, he was telling, "JT, STAND THE FUCK UP. GIVE ME ALL THE WEED AND ALL THE MONEY!" JT was leading the assailant to his mom's bedroom. His mom's bedroom was on the opposite side of the house. When she had her house built, she got the mother-in-law floor plan. The assailant didn't see me as a threat. He felt remorseful when he looked into my eyes.

Unsuspected

I don't think the assailant expected the children and I to be there. When I saw that JT and the assailant were in JT's mom's room, Jerome was walking from the den area into the living room. Jacob was still standing in the same place by the front door in the living room. I quickly gathered my two sons. I rushed them out the back door. Outside the back door was a porch that was fenced in with a wooden gate. I bent down to Jacob's level. I said, "Baby, don't come back in this house no matter what." A part of me wanted to take my children and run the opposite way. Then I thought to myself, *What if the assailant has accomplices? What if someone is waiting outside of the front door?* My mind went blank again. I was still in survival mode. I rushed back into the house from the back porch. As I was rushing back into the house, I heard JT's voice, he was yelling my name. He said, "I GOT HIM! I GOT HIM. COME BUST THIS NIGGA OVER HIS HEAD WITH SOMETHING."

I Ain't No Killer, but Don't Push Me

JT and the assailant were no longer in his mom's room. They somehow made their way back into the living room. They were tussling over the gun. They looked as if they were doing the tango. They tussled to the front door of the house. I was being sure to stay behind the barrow of the gun. I rushed toward the assailant that now looked like a black-and-white target. I proceeded to stab in the neck with the steak knife. His neck was thick like leather. Red blood started to pour out of the black-and-white target. I didn't feel anything. My adrenaline rushed, and blood continued to pour. Once I saw the blood pouring, something happened to my vision and senses. I could see in color. The steak knife seemed not to be effecting him. The assailant continued as if there was no blood pouring. JT and the assailant tussled out of the front door way of the house.

Bang

They bumped and banged against the walls of the house, leaving splats of blood everywhere. I continued running besides them stabbing the assailant in the neck. He continued like he didn't feel me stabbing. The final corner of the house met with the driveway. When they made it to the final corner of the house, the assailant was able to point the gun toward me. JT had his finger behind the trigger. I wasn't sure how long that would work. In a frantic mode to survive, I ran as fast as I could back into the house. I ran into the house. I ran to the backyard. I saw that the kids were still on the back porch. We ran into the den area. I shut the door to the den, then I locked it. As I turned the lock on the den door, I heard *POW, POW, POW, POW* along with some shattering of glass.

Relief

I didn't know what to think or expect. I told the kids to stay quiet. I found the house phone sitting on a corner table in the den. With this fearful feeling in my gut, I picked up the phone and dialed the numbers 9-1-1 with my right hand while holding the knife in my left. The operator picked up, she said, "911, do you need fire ambulance or police?" I said, "Help us. We are being robbed." The operator said, "Ma'am, officers are on the way. There have been many calls referring to your residence. Does someone there need EMS?" Then she said, "Do you think you can calm down and describe the perpetrator to me?"

Bang on the Door

I said yes but then I was startled by a bang on the door. I didn't know who it was. "Someone is banging on the door," I said. The operator said, "It's okay, honey. Those are officers. Stay on the phone with me while you open the door for them." I told my boys to stay in the den. I ran to the front door and looked out the peep hole. It was two officers. I opened the door for the officers. The first officer asked me if I was hurt and if there's anyone else inside of the home with me. I said, "Yes, I am here with my two sons." I heard the operator's voice through the phone and she said, "Hello?" The second officer grabbed the phone out of my hand and began speaking to the operator. While the second officer was speaking to the operator, the first officer noticed all the blood everywhere.

The Horror

There was blood all over my clothes arms and hands. I hadn't noticed it. The first officer asked where my sons were. I pointed to the den. The officer went to the den, opened the door, and retrieved my boys. He brought them to the living room where I was. We walked around the wall to the kitchen and sat at the dining table. The other officer walked into the kitchen hanging up the phone. The paramedics came in. They wanted to make sure the blood didn't belong to me or the children. The paramedics placed blood pressure cups on the children and me. They checked our blood pressure. Once they were done, they went back out the front door.

Crime Scene

When the paramedics went out, forensics came in. A man in a white lab coat and a kit in hand, walked over to the kitchen table with the boys and me. He pulled a test tube out of the kit. The test tube had some type of liquid and some Q-tips enclosed in it. Once he pulled the test tube out of his kit, he sat the kit on the table and sat in the chair beside me. He put some white gloves on, pulled the lid off the test tube, and pulled out one of the cotton swabs. Once he got the cotton swab out the test tube, he proceeded to run the Q-tip in between all my fingers. The Q-tip became soiled in blood and human skin. My hands and clothes were covered with assailant's blood and skin.

Over My Dead Body

When the forensic guy got done swabbing my fingers, he put the soiled Q-Tip into another test tube. Then he gathered his things and left out the front door. Victim Services came in with toys and bears to entertain the children. The police were taking statements from me about what happened. During everything going on, I noticed that JT hadn't come back in the house. Where was he? I thought back on the shots fired and the sound of shattering glass I heard earlier. Did he get shot? Was he dead? Everything that could possibly go through my mind went through my mind. I began to get anxiety. I asked the officers if they saw him out there. No one answered.

Where Was He?

I jumped up from the table. I had to go see what happened to the father of my children. I rushed to the front door. When I stepped out of the house on to the sidewalk, I could not believe the scene that was unfolding before me. I felt like I was on set of a gruesome horror movie. There was blood everywhere. The law enforcements had the entire place surrounded. When I looked at the wall of the house, I saw blood splat everywhere. It looked as if someone picked up a black cat, threw it up against the wall, and it made a big splat. I continued to walk down the sidewalk to the last corner of the house where the driveway met the house. I looked to the right to see forensics combing the grass. Forensics had numbers on white cards on the grass and on the driveway. Blood was even in the grass. The assailant or JT were nowhere in sight.

A Dead Body

I looked down toward the edge of the driveway. I saw an ambulance. As I got closer to the ambulance, I saw all the medics trying to help the person in the ambulance. Then I heard one of the medics say, "We lost him." My heart stopped. My jaw dropped. I knew it couldn't be anyone but JT. "Oh my God, help me! How was I going to explain this to my children?" I dropped to my knees. One of the medics came to my side to help me off the ground. She put an electric blanket over my shoulders. I felt numb. I was crying. The woman medic was telling me, "Everything is going to be okay."

Attempted Robbery

Then I felt another set of hands on my shoulders from the back. I heard a man voice say, "Everything is good." I turned to see his face. It was JT. He was okay. Unfortunately, the perpetrator remembered JT before he went to prison. He remembered all the money and drugs JT used to have and wanted a slice of the pie. When I heard the set of shots fired, JT and the perpetrator were fighting over the gun. JT removed his finger from behind the trigger. He said, "He kept a grip on the gun." They shot in the air. JT said, "He took off running while the second bullet was being dislodged from the gun." Then the assailant pointed the gun toward JT. Through the grace of God, the assailant shot and missed JT, but shot out the next-door neighbor's car window. No one was in the car.

Thoughts of Murder

The assailant shot off one rounder with hopes of killing JT. That was the final shot I heard. The assailant was so weak from loss of blood that he collapsed at the end of the driveway. I was so happy that JT was not the person in the back of the ambulance. We walked back into the house to unite with our children. When we went back into the house, I gathered my boys. I hugged and kissed them so tight. The authorities were still there gathering their evidence. A new officer arrived on the scene. I think he mentioned he was the sergeant. I don't quite remember. When he arrived, he asked for me by my first and last name. I was a little concerned that I would be the first person he wanted to speak to upon arrival. He told me I was a hero, and I did what I had to do to protect my family. He told me that this guy was responsible for a few other home invasions in the area. He also said that the same suspect broke into the home of an elderly couple and caused the husband to have a heart attack. He went on to say, "If there is ever a situation like this happen again, God forbid, but if it is, but if it ever—" He looked me right in the eye and said, "Take the knife, stick it right here." He pointed at the area of his chest beneath the nipple area. Then he said, "Twist and turn it, instant death." I could not believe the officer said that. He kind of gave me the creeps. Once the investigators and other law enforcement got everything they needed, they began to clear the scene. They were there for several hours gathering evidence. I was mentally and physically exhausted. Once the scene was clear, I started to clear out. I gathered my children's things. We went home. After all the battles in my life and finally getting life back on track, here we were reaping the consequence of our past.

Home Safe

Many things on my mind. I could not believe what we just went through. It was so surreal. When I pulled up to my driveway, I reversed my car into the driveway. I wanted everything around me set up for easy access or escape. That home invasion really messed up my mind. I opened my car door to get out. I shut the door behind myself leaving the children in the car. I used my key alarm to lock the children in the car. They fell asleep while I was driving home. I was traumatized. I became squeamish. A car pulled on my street with headlights on, I became fearful. The car was almost a mile away but it was creeping slow. It was late. There weren't many cars out that late. Something didn't seem right. I panicked and ran to the front door of my house. I put the key in the lock and turned it. I ran quickly to the kitchen. I opened the cabinet over the stove.

My Girlfriend

That was where I kept my gun. I grabbed my gun. The gun was fully loaded. I loaded it when I got out of the shelter. Then I stashed it on the top shelf where the children couldn't reach it. I quickly ran back out to my car. I used my key alarm to unlock the car door. I quickly jumped in my car and locked the car doors. As the car lights got closer, the front of the car looked familiar. I saw it when I was on the highway driving home. But when I made a couple of quick turns, the car disappeared. I figured, I was just being paranoid because of what had just occurred. But now, I knew I wasn't mistaking. This was the same car that I thought I'd lost on I-35. Someone was following me. The car continued driving toward my driveway. I was trembling. I didn't know if someone was coming back to retaliate. It was dark. I couldn't see what the make or model of the car was. All I could see was headlights. I put my key in the ignition. I quickly cranked my car. I threw the gear stick in drive and sped toward the end of the driveway. My intent was to drive to a more secure lit up area or to a police station. The car pulled in my driveway blocking me in. I made sure the safety was off my gun. I had my Sunday night special girlfriend locked and loaded. After the day I had, I was ready to kill again.

Who Is in This Car?

When the car came to a halt, someone in the car started flashing the bright lights on and off. Who the fuck was this. They were in straight violation, and I had a big surprise for them. I was about to light their asses up. After the high beams flashed on for the fifth time, they went off. This time they went all the way to the park lights. I could see two people in the front seat of the car, but the driver was a woman. The passenger was a man. The passenger side door opened. I could see the man stepping out of the car. When he stood up out of the car, I had my gun pointed at him. I played it all out in my head. I thought, *I will let him get close enough so that I can make sure I don't miss. This motherfucker done followed me to my house. He is going to get it.* As he walked closer, my heart beat faster. With every step he took, my hearing became intensified. I could hear his footsteps. When he got close enough, I heard his voice say, "Where are you going this time of night?" I lowered the gun because I knew this voice. As he walked closer, a glare from the street light glimpsed upon his face. My brain did a scan over his face and analyzed his voice like a computer with voice and face recognition.

Familiar

It was my children's father. I put the safety on the gun and put in the glove box and locked it. Then I unlocked my car doors. JT opened my car door. He stood at the window long enough to see me putting the safety on the gun, and he saw when I locked it away in the glove box. JT asked, "Was that a gun?" I said, "Hell yeah." Although I was scared as hell, I had never been happier to see him. Shortly after I drove away, JT's mom drove up to her house. He caught her up on what just occurred. He asked his mom to drive him to my house to check on the boys. I asked him if they were behind me on I-35. He said yes. I said, "But then y'all disappeared." I thought, *I lost y'all*. He said, "We stopped at the gas station to get gas. I knew what street you lived on because one of my friends told me they saw you taking groceries out of the car and into your house." Then he said, "I told mama to drive slow. I was looking for your car. I wouldn't have seen your car had it not been for the automatic lights. When you cranked the car, the lights came on. That is when I knew which house you stayed in." I was like, "Oh okay." I told JT to sit in the car with the boys, and then I went over to speak to JT's mom. She wanted to see her grandbabies to make sure they were okay.

Checking on the Grandbabies

I told her that they were in the car sleeping. She got out of her car and walked to my car. She checked on the babies. She gave them kisses. She told me that she was just bringing JT to check on me and the children, but it was time for her to get back home. She asked JT if he was going to stay the night. That question threw me for a loop. I thought to myself, *How is she gone ask him something that she should've asked me?* Then JT said, "Ty, would you mind if I spent the night?" Under the circumstances, I said yeah. I didn't want to make a big fuss about it in front of his mom, but I wasn't expecting that. JT's mom got in her car and drove off. I told JT to reverse my car back into my driveway close to the door. I walked up the grass to my door. JT drove up the driveway. I walked up to the door. In a paranoid manner, I looked all around me making sure no one was to my left or right as I was putting my key in the door. When I got the door unlocked, I walked back out to the car.

Take the Strap Out the Glove

I unlocked the glove box and took my gun out of the box. I walked back into the house before. I was trying to put the gun back in the hiding space without JT seeing where I had put it. When I went back outside to help him bring the boys in, he was still trying to figure out the booster and car seat. I laughed at him. Big bad JT didn't know how to take his own baby out of a car seat. It was cute in a way. I showed him how to unlock the car seat and the booster seat. JT carried Jacob inside, and I carried Jerome inside. I showed JT to the boy's bedroom. He lay Jacob down in his bed and kissed him good night. Once I lay Jerome down his bed, JT walked over to his bed and kissed him good night. Then I turned on their night lights in their room. I walked out of the boy's room. JT followed. I was very drained mentally and physically. I was hungry, but I couldn't bring myself to eat anything. I walked the floors for twenty minutes. JT was sitting in the living area on the couch in the dark.

Paranoid and Tripping

I was a paranoid wreck. I felt anxiety building up in my chest. I kept checking all the doors and the locks. JT sat there calmly in the dark. I didn't know how he was keeping it together so well. I guess he got tired of seeing me pace the floors. I walked to the window to peek out for the twentieth time. JT walked over to the window where I was standing. He grabbed me by my hand and said, "Relax." He guided me back into the living room. He was motioning for me to have a seat on the couch. Once I was seated, he sat. I had on a pair of sandals that buckled all the way up to my calf. When JT sat me on the couch, he pulled my feet up in his lap. Then he said, "These Jesus's sandals are pretty tight." I said, "Ha-ha, funny!" There were seven buckles that he had to undo to take the shoe off. He unbuckled each buckle. He pulled my shoes off and sat them besides the couch. I lay down on the couch while he began to massage my feet. I felt really tired, but I was uncomfortable in my flesh. I was starting to feel frantic.

Order My Steps

I kept trying to put the events of the day in an order that made sense. In my head, I played the timeline of that whole day over and over. I couldn't figure it out. How could this happen. I was no longer indulged in that kind of living. Why would it happen to us now? Now that I was choosing to live my life right. I blamed JT. He assured and secured me that he was no longer in that life. He promised me that I would never have to worry about him taking that route ever again in life. He went on forty-five minutes or so. He emphasized on assuring and securing me. He told me his dreams, plans, and goals and all of the goals, plans, and dreams included bettering himself and being a better person to me and the children. JT stopped massaging my feet and pulled his shoes off. He put the shoes on the side of the couch next to my shoes. Then he slid up to where I was and lay behind me. We talked for hours. It seemed like we'd been talking all night. He started a reminiscing session to take my mind off the home invasion.

Good Memories

We got so consumed in the good memories of our past that I almost forgot that seven hours earlier we almost lost our lives. I must admit, I was having a good time with JT. He wrapped his arms around me from behind. It felt so good. It felt like it felt when I was in love with him before we gave birth to the children. He reminded me of the mild-mannered JT I met at the barbecue place I used to work at. I felt like I'd been placed in a time machine and being allowed time and space to redo the past. JT smelled so good. Everything about him was so familiar. It was a good familiar. He kissed me on the back of my neck. I felt my whole body shake. I was feeling weak for him. At that moment, I didn't want him to know that. So, I played it cool. I acted as if I didn't notice that he kissed me gently. I forgot about that kind of interaction. Yes, over the years there were a few conversations with other guys. I'd been so busy trying to regain myself positively and purposely. I'd neglected human relationships outside of what me and the children had.

No Trust and No Love

I didn't trust anyone. I never let anyone get too close. JT kissed the back of my neck again. This time the kiss was longer and warmer. He knew me, so he knew all the ways to touch me and get to me. I tried to ignore the kiss again. I closed my eyes tight to picture something that could take my mind into another focus. He kissed again and hugged me close. This time I couldn't contain myself. I heard myself inhale. I made a sighing sipping air sound. I hoped he didn't hear me, but I knew he did. I quickly opened my eyes. I turned to position myself on my back. He remained laying on his side. Now we were face to face. I didn't know what to expect. I just hoped that he would ignore my body language. I was afraid of the past. I told myself I would never be with him again. I knew him and what he was capable of. In a trembling voice, I said "I'm scared. I haven't been with anyone else." I went on to explain everything I felt when he was choking me.

The Promise

He promised me that who he was when he was on drugs was not him. He assured me that he would never do drugs again, and he would never be that same person again. He told me that he got saved when he was incarcerated. He said that he had been working on his relationship with God. Then he said he missed his family a lot. He also said he realized where he went wrong, and now he wanted to fix everything that he did wrong. I looked into his eyes. I said, "I am scared." He hugged and kissed me. His lips penetrated my lips deeply. I could feel the warmth of his breath and how soft his lips were. When I pulled my lips away from his, it felt as if we were unsticking. He said, "Put your trust in God and he will guide you and I will protect you. Please let me love you." He leaned forward to kiss me again. We kissed passionately. JT scooted off the couch. He stood up on to his feet. He leaned down picking me up in a swooping manner. He lifted me up off the couch. He continued to kiss me. JT began walking with me. I felt as if I was floating in midair.

Knocks Me Off My Feet

I didn't see where we were going, but I felt myself gliding across the room. He carried me into my bedroom. We were in a state of euphoria. He continued kissing me so passionately. He hugged me so tight. I wrapped my arms around him hugging him tighter. He released my legs to dangle as if he was trying to put me down so that my feet could touch the floor. When my feet touched the floor, he pulled off his shirt. I placed my hand on his chest where his heart is and glided my fingertips over his nicely chiseled physique. I said, "Jail got you yoked up, boy. You been hitting them waits." He pulled me close to him at the waist. I had on a spaghetti strap dress. He gazed into my eyes. I didn't see his hands, but I felt his hand slid my right strap off my shoulder. Then I felt the other strap fell off my shoulders. The dress fell to the floor. He picked me up. I locked my legs around his waist to insure security. He lay me down on the bed. Behind him, I saw out of my window a full moon lit the nights sky. By this time, I was lost in the sauce of love. I'd lost all control. I no longer had any worries or fears. Hell, I no longer had any control. Every thought that plagued me earlier were no longer relevant.

I Want Him

From that moment on, I knew he was the one I wanted to spend the rest of my life with. He put it down! I felt fulfilled mentally, spiritually, and emotionally. He made sure he placed me securely on the bed as if I was as fragile as glass and delicate as a flower. He began to kiss me on my forehead. He kissed from my forehead down to my nose and then to my lips. He sucked my neck gently but firmly. Then he kissed down to my chest onto my breast. I was so turned on. By the time he reached my breast, my nipples were protruding. He paid special attention to each individual breast. He slightly sucked on my nipples. I could feel the warmth of his tongue and breath on my nipples. While suckling my nipples, he grazed the flat of his tongue on my nipples in a slow circular motion. I was about to lose my mind. Everything was so perfect. In my head I started thanking God for such a perfect moment and such a perfect guy. I was in love again. Just as I was in our earlier years. He pulled his pants off. When I saw his penis, it startled me. I thought, *How is that going to fit in this?* I forgot what he looked like down there. The more he kissed, I felt bliss. I became one with the blanket and the bed. I felt like I was melting. My vagina flowed like the ocean. He hugged me tighter. My fears became lighter. He continued kissing and licking in a circular motion. When he got down to my vagina, he licked and sucked on my clitoris.

This Is Love

He kissed and loved it like he had been thinking about treating it the best way he could. I didn't remember it feeling so good. After ten minutes of ultimate passion, he rubbed the tip of his penis at the opening of my vagina. He looked surprised and amazed by the ocean flow. I guess he was getting a refresher course of how good the punani was too. I knew about the sexual response cycle and how it worked. Not only did I know what was going on with my body and his, I felt it and saw it. The increased released endorphins intensified. He began to push in the opening of my vagina slowly. I felt like a virgin all over again. He said, "Oh my, it is so tight. You weren't lying. This my PUSSY and it always will be." He continued to push and stroke gently. With each stroke, I seductively moaned louder and longer. He moaned. We moaned until climax. I screamed, and he groaned. We reached our release point at the same time. I fell fast asleep. I slept well with no worries. I woke up the next morning, and he was already awake. He was watching me sleeping. When I opened my eyes, he rubbed my face and said, "Good morning, beautiful." I said, "Good morning." I had no regrets. I was glad that he and his mom had followed me home. I was glad he stayed the night.

Breakfast in Bed

JT got out of bed. He was already dressed. I put my dress back on. I went to the bathroom to freshen up. I went back to my bedroom. JT was sitting on my bed with freshly made breakfast. He sat next to me. He put his hand on my vagina and said, "Do you remember when I said this is my pussy and always will be?" I said yes. He said, "I mean that." He stooped down on the side of the bed. He was down on both knees. He reached his hand up to me. I put my hand in his hand. While pulling my hand downward, he asked me to get down there beside him on both knees. I got down on the floor beside him on both knees. He said, "All right. Now bow your head." I bowed my head. He started praying. He said, "Father God, I come to you with a humble heart. God, you know I love this woman and the children you gave to me. Will you please bless us to go forward as one body with you. If you honor this God, guide her heart." Then he turned to me and said, "Ty, I've love you from the day I met you. I never want to go through good day or bad days with anyone else in this world but you. Will you please be my forever love and happiness?" I usually have to play the outcomes of things and calculate the what ifs in life and in a situation. At that moment, I was so sure. I was surer at that moment than I had ever been in any other moment in my life. I said, "Yes. I love you so much." Six months later, we had an extravagant wedding where we were married. A year later, I owned my own beauty school, and he was doing well in real estate. We were a spiritually growing family with our first little girl on the way.

About the Author

Tasha Brooks is an inventor, author, writer, performer, singer, artist, and an analytical thinker. She's born and raised in the city of Austin, which is the capital of Texas. She was given the gifts of spiritual insight and empathy. These gifts enable her to become one with individuals. Becoming one with individual's character traits allows her to get in to character. From when Tasha was a small child, she realized she possessed these gifts. She can emulate and portray someone's life emotions and circumstances with intricate detail. The intricate detail brings real situations and characters to life. Characters that paint pictures and books with vivid color. Tasha's favorite thing to do is to people watch. Through people watching, she soaks up and analyzes ways of living, hurting, loving, and dealing. She is a good interpreter of predicting different outcomes to situations with accuracy. Often, she has been sarcastically accused of being a psychic. Tasha knows she's not a psychic. She is an enthusiastic, optimistic individual of ambitions that listens to her inner spiritual self. (Obedience.) She says that one will find that, when we listen to that insight, everything will line up right. Tasha feels that her purpose is to become a platform and a voice for thinkers and singers that have a song or a story but are afraid to sing or speak. This writer will be the bridge to glory.

CPSIA information can be obtained
at www.ICGtesting.com
Printed in the USA
LVHW090227200819
628263LV00002B/222/P